EVOLVE

OVERCOMING THE PAIN AND
FAILURES OF YOUR PAST

DR. LEGACY

authorHOUSE®

AuthorHouse™
1663 Liberty Drive
Bloomington, IN 47403
www.authorhouse.com
Phone: 833-262-8899

Published by AuthorHouse 09/21/2020

ISBN: 978-1-6655-0098-2 (sc)
ISBN: 978-1-6655-0143-9 (e)

Print information available on the last page.

This book is printed on acid-free paper.

Scripture taken from the King James Version of the Bible.

In Loving memory of my grandparents who helped raise me and introduced me to Jesus Christ. I will never forget you all. There is not a day that goes by that you all are not in my thoughts. Being your grandson and a member of your church was the greatest thing that could have ever happened to me. Although the membership of your church was exceedingly small the congregation never went over twenty people, but little did you know that the boy you were raising up would reach hundreds even thousands. The faith and hope you placed in me will never die, the dreams and visions you stirred in me will never be abandoned. Because of you, I am. And I will always speak your names and I will always tell the world who you are to me. I love you all the way into the heavens.

Your grandson

I would like to dedicate this book to all of those who deal with depression, bipolar disorder, PTSD, anxiety, and other mental illnesses. This book is for those who wear a smile daily, laugh and say that everything is okay when in private they are broken and torn. For these are the ones that are often looked over and forgotten but find the strength to create and make life better for others but have yet to find their happy place in this world.

I pray that this book helps you give your pain a voice. It is my prayer that every word in this book is a gift to your soul and repair the broken places in your life. I pray that each chapter you read gives you the strength to change and transform into a better you. And for those who have suffered in life and trying to figure it all out because of the abuse and rejection you have endured, this was written for you as well.

Please know that there is life after pain and your worst setback can become your greatest victory when you trust the power within yourself. It is in these pages you will find out that every ugly and shameful thing you had to face was not placed in your life to kill and to destroy you, but it happened to position you for your greatest evolution. For those that are in the middle of a battle in life now, please know that your life is not falling apart but it is falling in place.

INTRODUCTION

Never was the smartest person in the room at least that is how I felt about myself anyway. Graduated with a special Ed. Diploma with a 1.8 GPA. I could only read on a fifth-grade level when I walked off the graduation field. Yet I was so full of hope and life. The black and gold tassel dangles in the win as I smiled running across the field with that special education diploma inside the leatherback portfolio. I held it up high in the sky I was so proud of myself. I was dyslexic but proud, rejected but proud, lost but proud, knowing that things were going to get better for me. I was told by my teachers that I would never go to college and that the only job I was able to get and will ever have was either flipping burgers or working in a nearby warehouse.

Life became so real to me after that. I married a year later. No job, no money, no home, not even a car. I was beyond broke. Twenty years old full of hopes and dreams that things would get better. But it seemed like the more I believed the harder life got and the harder it got the more people talked and the more people talked the more discouraged I became.

I had fallen in love with this beautiful young girl from the church I attended. Her and I had been together throughout all my high school years. Outside of my grandparents she was the one that I truly trusted and loved and one who I knew without doubt loved and honored me no despite what others said. She saw me through the eyes of God and when you find love like that you don't abuse it or take it for granted you hold dear to it and embrace it with all you soul and might. And that is what I did in the beginning. We were all one another had. It appears the whole world was against us and we fought hard to do all we could to make life work. The day my wife found out she was carrying our first child it was a heavy but hopeful day. Our dreams faded in the win. We became discouraged we were not ready to take care of another life we could barely afford to breath and now this new life had come to us like a thief in the night.

My wife laying on the backroom cot in the doctor's office, the room was bright with one weak flickering lightbulb going in and out. We held each other's hand having just gotten the news that we were expecting a child. The midwife reached overtook the heart monitor and placed it on my wife's belly and the sound of a small heartbeat echoed through the room like a kick of a beating drum. The anxiety and worry that had arrested my wife and I vanished in that very moment. For we had been so scared about becoming parents for the first time. It was not what we had planned so early in our life, but it was something about hearing that baby's heartbeat that changed our perspective about the change we were about to embark upon. It is funny how a single sound can shift your emotions and thoughts of hopelessness into thoughts and acts of faith. We were so overwhelmed with fear and doubt that we forgot about all the positive things that a child could bring into our world. Our surroundings had led us to believe that our lives were over and that our hopes and dreams of being successful was out the door.

Oh, how untrue that was but anything can become true when you believe it long enough. What you believe creates the world around you. Your faith and your fears are lenses in which how you see the world. Let me be real with you, I have heard it all. I was told that I was not good enough I was too black, too ugly, too loud too skinny was not smart enough. I was told that I did not come from the right family and because of the bad things my family did I did not have it in me to be greater than them. Many times, I listened to those voices and at times I believed them because of my own insecurities but as I grew and time passed, I realized that those that spoke such things to me were battered people who had lost all hope for themselves and could not see hope in me.

You can't expect acceptance from a self-battered individual. I had to learn how to listen to the heartbeat of hope that echoed out through that back room of that doctor's office and find peace in the life God has given us. My wife looked at me and smiled as we all listened to the beat of that baby's heart. Nothing else mattered at that moment. I remember looking at my wife square in the eyes and without a sound proceeding out of my mouth using only my lips I mouthed, I love you. What was beating and growing inside her was giving life to the dead things people had spoken over us. But most of all that little baby was evolving into a little person that would cause our family to grow. We did not plan this neither did we want this, but God gave it to us and after hearing that baby's heart we accepted the plan of God.

Although I had been overwhelmed in doubt and fear something in me believed that everything was going to be ok. I could no longer allow anyone to have space in my life that was not for me and the hard part of it all, I had to learn to love me, all of me. I had to stop making excuses and start accepting who I was in this life. I been through it all, the self-loathing the self-pity the shame and embarrassment and I had to put an end to it. That heartbeat of hope that came from the belly of my wife gave me a broader view of what life was about. I could have listened to those that told us that we were too young to be having a child and that we were too young to be married all of what was being said could have been true but the outcome of it all has such a bigger meaning. All of this said one thing to me, and that one thing was changed.

Change is good when you're controlling the wheel of life and it is all going according to the way you planned it but what do you do when change comes unexpectedly? What happens when you must deal with things that you did not plan? Do you ignore it? Do you give up and stop fighting? Do you accept it all and make the best of the worst? situation and trust that God has your heart in His hand, and He will never take you through something He can't get you out of.

I do not know about you, but I choose the latter. It is not easy I know it is not, but how long will you keep being a victim? How long will you be a loser? How long will you be slothful and lazy about doing what you must do to make life work? You come too far to stop fighting now. Why get here to this point in your life and stop going after your dreams don't you know that once you stop fighting for what you want, what you don't want is bound to take over when will you stop lying to yourself and telling yourself that, "it's always going to be like this, nothing will never happen for me." The biggest lie of all is, "I can't do this." How long will you keep telling yourself, "life isn't fair and I'm not good enough"?

I challenge you as you read this book to listen for the heartbeat listen for the pulse because in that is the sound of life and where there is life there is hope and where there is hope there is faith and where there is faith there is change and change is always necessary for those that are bound to be great. You are going to have to shut down all negativity and dismiss all of those that do not hear the heartbeat of hope in your life. Rid yourself of selective hearing people. These are people that are deaf to the heartbeat of success in your life, but they hear the silent whispers and rumors of your faults and failures.

You are bigger than you think you are believing that, the most important person to believe in is yourself. Go after that and change your surroundings. You are your biggest responsibility if you can change you, you can change the world. Become someone you never been before. For once in your life go against the grain. Become what they said you will never become prove them wrong. Know that there will never be a shortage of people that want to see you fail you will never run out of haters and naysayers. Although your enemies may be large in number they are small in their minds. What is in you is greater than what they think or have to say about you, even if it is true.

Do not allow your weaknesses to define you. Outlive your mistakes overcome your failures and outlast the lies and the rumors. Minimize your proclivities and maximize your merits this is your season of evolution. Own what happen to you, own what you did and did not do, own who you are and embrace who you are to be. Stop allowing your past mistakes to manipulate you into giving up on your life. Everything happens for a reason know that it happens for you not to you. You are someone's miracle that is getting ready to happen. What I am simply saying my beloved is to EVOLVE. Be unstoppable in all that you do knowing that you are opening a whole new future for you and for those that are connected to you. In this book I will be incredibly open and transparent about my life and provide not only words of wisdom for you to overcome but personal testimonials to let you know that you are not alone. I believe that trust and transformation is birthed out of transparency. I pray that as I share my life with you and as I share my words with you that you become another person. This is your hour of evolution walk in it become it be it.

CHAPTER 1

YOU MATTER

+ + + + + + +

"I will praise thee; for I am fearfully and wonderfully made:
marvellous are thy works; and that my soul knoweth right well."

—Psalm 139:14, King James Version

The steps squeaked softly as I made my way up the stairs headed for bed. The house was dark, only the light of my television shined through the small hallway of that two bedrooms apartment. The smell of cigarettes stained the air as the smoke creeped out of the other room. I sighed with relief as I walked through my bedroom door. Turning on my light I began to take off my Sunday clothes preparing to go to bed. It had been a long Sunday night and all I wanted to do was lay down and watch the Grammys. It was the same year Kirk Franklin won an award for best gospel album of the year with the song "STOMP" I slowly laid across the bed that set only on a broken box spring on the floor.

Laying there looking at the television my door slowly opened creaking on its hinges. I turned and saw that it was him coming in to talk to me. With nothing but his underwear on he laid beside me spooning me telling me that he loved me in a tired but sleepy voice I replied, "I love you too." After about thirty minutes I fell asleep in his arms. An hour or two had passed when I woke up to find this man's hand in my underwear. I pushed away and within that moment he put his hand over my mouth and attack me. The smell of booze was on his breath and his skin reeked with the smell of marijuana and cigarette smoke. He laid on top of me and began to spit on my bottom several times like I was nothing as if my body were a dirty ground and he was the one above it, walks on it as well as defiling it with his waste. Forcing himself on me I felt the worst pain I had ever felt in my life. I tried screaming but by this time he had me face down in the mattress so every sound that proceeded out of my mouth was muffled and faint, I could barely breathe. He ravished me for over thirty minutes although it felt like hours. I felt like someone had reached up inside me and pulled out my soul. I was in so much pain my body shook on its on accord trying to figure out this foreign torture that was being placed on it. Drops of his sweat fell on my back he grunted and breathed heavy as he continued to rape and molest me. When he was done, he pulled me close to him with his lips touching the tip of my ear he whispered to me, "If you tell anyone they will take you away from this family and you will never see your grandparents again and you can forget about going to church and singing and preaching all of that will be over. Who will believe you anyway everyone knows that you're gay and that you are a little faggot. So, if I was you I would keep my mouth shut."

From that day on I shut down on the inside never to utter a word of it to anyone. He got up and left the room sly and slowly just as he had entered hours before. I broke down crying pulling myself up from the frameless bed I made my way to the bathroom, I could barely walk. Bleeding and sobbing my thirteen-year-old body was shaking and scared. I turned the shower on to wash off the fluids and smell of the monster that had attacked me. For two years this went on at least two to three times a week. It got so bad that I no longer fought it, I lost all strength and power to push it away I began to embrace the abuse and respect the abuser it was the only way I could survive without losing my mind. There were days I would scream and cry out to God and beg Him to kill me, "take my life" I would say with tears falling down my face but God gave a deaf ear to my cry.

By the time I was fourteen years old I had grown depressed and was failing every class in school I was bullied and called names every day. I found no acceptance no matter where I turned. Even in the church the young people made fun of me because I would come to church and shout out of clothes screaming and crying out to God in hopes that He would hear me and see me and change the pain that was tormenting me within. Although they picked at me no one knew the pain that I faced at home. My life seemed to have no value. I was confused about everything. I did not know who I was or why I existed. I began to feel like maybe I am not supposed to be happy. I loved church I loved to preach and sing because that was the only time I seemed to be accepted and loved outside of the bed of abuse I face behind closed doors. I hated myself so much by the time I was sixteen I had tried to take my own life at least five times. This was the beginning of the days I would like to call The Great Unknown.

After every suicide attempt, I would wake up and come to myself and ask God, "Why?" Why are you allowing me to suffer like this? Why am I here? Why no one loves me? Why do not I matter to anyone? It took me years to receive the answer to those questions. I had to survive the problems in order to receive and accept the answers. After some time had passed, I grew and so, did the power within me. I began to fight off my abuser and the more I would fight him the less he came after me. I grew tired of the pain and the false allusions of love and affection. I moved out of that house and moved in with my grandparents who were pastors, strong Pentecostal holiness preachers who loved the Lord and who loved me. After escaping the abuse my faith in God became my bread and meat for survival. Church was all I did. Singing and preaching became a way of escape from the terrible truth that had happened to me. I thought maybe if I preached real hard shouted wild and loud maybe the pain would go away. But I was sadly mistaken. After every church service and every prayer meeting, I was left alone with a battle of feeling unloved feeling unwanted and feeling abandoned.

For you see although I had left the geographic location where I was abused the residue of the abuse never left me. Often times those that are abused deal with the overwhelming feeling of rejection and loneliness and you feel like no matter what you do you will never be good enough. When you have been abused it strips you of your self-worth and leaves a whole and a gap in your soul that cannot be filled. This is why many turns to addictions and substance abuse because they are trying to fill the gap in their soul that was placed there by someone who took advantage of them. Many turn to sexual immoral abusing their bodies trying to make sense of it all. I almost got stuck after this horrific event in my life.

I began to turn to porn and solicited sex from people that I did not even know. Jumping in and out of windows sleeping with strangers in cars in the woods behind abandon buildings. I had become the product of what was placed upon me by someone that was supposed to take care of me and love me. I almost got stuck. This young Pentecostal preacher began to hang out with the wrong crowd. I found myself in bars picking up individuals just to have sex. By the time I was nineteen I had multiple sex partners some of them I didn't even know their names. I was living a holy sanctified life by day but a life of darkness and sexual perversion by night.

My abuser did not only teach me how to keep a secret, but he taught me how to lie and live a life of a hypocrite. It all came to a head one Thursday night I was on my way to bible study after getting high with some friends I got in the car with my mother. By this time, my grandmother had died and went home to be with the Lord and my cousin the Pastor had taken over the church. I walked in bible study that night just as high as I wanted to be. I seat in the back eyes red as fire I slumped down in the pew trying to hide the fact that I had smoked a joint with my peers. When Bible study ended that night Pastor said, "Would anyone like to say anything before we dismiss?" First Lady got up slowly from the bench she had been sitting on. With her right hand raised in the air clutching her bible to her chest with her left hand she said, "Pastor, I have something I would like to say." "Go ahead" the Pastor replied. Like an angry witness in a courtroom accusing the defendant First Lady pointed at me and shouted out my name. She called me by name and said loud, "whatever you been doing and whatever you have involved yourself with God said No! He has a plan for your life and what you have been practicing is not His perfect will for you." She went on to say, "Son I know you been hurt, and I know you been broken but this is not the answer what God has for you is greater than what you're going through. I know you feel like you do not matter because no one has told you that you do matter but Legacy I came to tell you that you do matter and your life won't end like this!" "Stand up", she said, "Let me lay my hands on you." Full of shame guilt and condemnation I lifted myself up from the pew with tears in my eyes and my hands lifted towards Heaven I broke down and cried. She walked towards the back of the church where I was standing in a hurry as if she was coming to give me something and she slapped her hand on my forehead and rebuked the devil that had been tormenting me. After praying over me in the Holy Ghost she hugged me and told me, "Legacy" God's hand is on your life boy, He's going to use you for His glory you matter to Him, don't give up baby." The feeling of hope and love filled me that night. It was one of the greatest feelings I had ever felt in my life. I knew what pain felt like I knew what sex felt like I knew what being high and drunk felt like and this feeling exceeded all of those. It was a feeling of belonging and self-acceptance I found myself in God that night. That God moment repositioned me to another place in life.

"And I will put enmity between thee and the woman, and between thy seed and her seed; it shall bruise thy head, and thou shalt bruise his heel." (Genesis 3:15, KJV). As we study the history of the bible, we will see that even in Exodus Satan filled Pharaoh's heart to kill all the male children because he had to stop Moses from coming. "And Pharaoh charged all his people, saying, Every son that is born ye shall cast into the river, and every daughter ye shall save alive" (Exodus 1:22, KJV).

In Matthew 2:16-18 Herod kills all the male children from 0-3years of age because he was trying to get to Jesus. But when God's hand is on your life cannot a devil in Hell take it off. The very fact that you survived the worst of life is a sign from the Heavens to let you know that you matter. God did not create you to suffer and be miserable all of your life, but He made you with a plan and purpose in mind. Like me you probably never felt accepted or wanted in this life and it feels like all you seem to get out of life is pain. But that is the lie of the enemy. There is something in you that caused you to survive it all and that something is called purpose. The days of the unknown were my teenage years and those are the days I seem to just be existing. Not knowing who I was and who I was to become. The enemy had interrupted my life with molestation, sexual immoral, drug abuse, alcohol abuse, and religion. All these things were a web of lies sent to me to distract me from my true self. There were days that I was strong and full of hope and I could stand what life was throwing at me. Then there were days that I could not even catch my breath from the inward struggle I had inside and in those days, God was holding me up so I would not fall. At this moment I want you to stop reading and take a deep breath and say to yourself, "I MATTER." I want you to keep saying it until you believe it, I want you keep saying it until that pain within you go away, say it until you feel the presence of the Almighty God. Come on do it now!

If God had not used First Lady to interrupt my days of the unknown, I would still be unknown. Drinking, smoking, and abusing myself with people that do not love me. Today I want to be to you what First Lady was to me that night, a way out and tell you that you matter. I know life has done you wrong but beloved, you matter. The sound of your past is louder than the sound of your future but its ok because, you matter. Your past would not be so loud if it wasn't threatened by the victory of your future. I know you feel thrown away and forgotten but my friend please know this, your feelings are lying to you.

You are not forgotten you are not looked over God is preparing you for something greater. You matter. I want to interrupt your days of the unknown and pull you out of that dark cloud of despair and let you know that you are loved you are beautiful you are gifted you are graced by a God that has ordered your steps and stops. He put a strength in you that not even your greatest enemy can take away. Look back over your life and think about all that you faced and look where you are right now. My friend, my beloved you made it through. There is a power in you that you do not even know you have. Tap into it lean on it and embrace it for it is that same power that will get you through what you are facing right now. You are not going to die like this.

People that matter does not die in dark days they live through them. And sometimes things must get worse before they get better but please know this, that the worst is over, and the best has arrived. The truth is you will never win in life by being someone you are not. The pain in your life often time tries to get you to deny who you really are and submit to a lesser broke down version of you. You cannot be successful by settling and not growing from who you use to be or what has happened to you. You will never be happy if you do not change how you view yourself. Until you accept and embrace who you are you will become destined to live an unhappy life. It's impossible to be genuinely happy if you are not genuinely yourself. If you want to walk in your full potential and fulfill your purpose in life you have got to know that it is okay to be you.

It does not matter who do not like you or who will not have your back trust me when I tell you, The right people will show up when the real you come forth. You are so incredibly special. There is no one like you in this whole world. God made one original you and there will never be anyone like you ever again, not in this age or even in the ages to come. Being yourself is the greatest power you can ever use in this world. Being yourself quickly filters out all the individuals that do not belong in your life and at the same time it reveals those that do. Who are you? I am not asking about your work, your job or who you want people to see, but who are you at the core? Knowing this gives you absolute power and control over your own destiny. Never be ashamed of who you are or where you come from. No matter what has happened to you, no matter where you come from, no matter what race you are or what your sex is, no matter what you believe learn to be yourself and treat others the way you would like to be treated.

If you do these things your life will become so easy to live. If you do not, life will be miserable and painful, and you will never be great. It is hard to live a life with a mask on because in doing so it cuts off the oxygen of the real amazing you. Being what you think people want you to be is a life lived under a curse. Living a life trying to be someone else, to make others happy it may bring temporary satisfaction on the outside but on the inside you will never be complete. I thought something was wrong with me the reason why I was molested. I thought it happened to me because of how I looked or acted. I went years thinking it was my fault. The pain of this act caused me to become a person I was not.

I wore a mask for years because I felt like if I really revealed myself to those I loved or to those I admired I would not be accepted. It took me years to get rid of that worthless feeling of being unwanted. It took me years to realize that there was nothing wrong with me but there was something wrong with the individuals that abused me. Growing up as a child you did not have a voice or a say so as a child. You were seen not heard. I remember finally coming forth telling the truth about what had happened to me and I did not get support at all. No one believed me. Many chose to believe the voice of the Violator more than they did the Victim. So, I shutdown. And I hated I ever open my mouth about it. I felt like I never mattered. It is funny but I felt like people loved the fake me and rejected the real me but in the end, I found out that the people that loved the fake me were fake people and the people that loved the real me were real people. Realness is the light of you that will eliminate the fake unauthentic darkness around you. I had to learn that I mattered. Even if the whole world turned against me, I had to find my voice during this dark world and know that there was nothing about me that did not carry some type of power.

You matter, regardless of what they say. You matter, regardless of what they think, you matter, regardless of what they may try and do to you. The action of your enemies will never overtake the power of God that is in you. We have come this far in life not just to survive the pain of it all but to conquer the shame of it all. My beloved you matter. You are not what they did to you, you are not what they say about you. You are stronger than any negative thing that has ever happened to you. So, pull yourself up dust yourself off and move beyond that place of brokenness.

What the devil wants is for you to park at the place of pain, but I am writing to you to tell you that you are parked in the wrong place. Allow this chapter to be your citation and ticket to alert you that you are no longer allowed to park in the place of pain but move from there and go beyond the struggle for in that you will see that all that has happened to you in the unknown God will make it right and make it work out for your good. Be committed to being yourself and speak your truth at all times even if they hate you. I need you to become comfortable with being hated for the truth than to be loved for a lie. You may come to a place in life where you give up and you fall but whatever you do, do not give up on you and do not allow yourself to fall. You are all you have in the end know that embrace that and operate in that. You are not being selfish by doing these things but you are being selfless. Take care of you and the world will be drawn to your needs and you will find yourself in a happy place of satisfaction.

CHAPTER 2

OVERCOMING REJECTION

+ + + + + + +

"When my father and my mother forsake me,

then the LORD will take me up."

— Psalm 27:10, KJV

There are three types of people reading this book right now.

1. People that have been rejected.

2. People that are going through rejection

3. People that are about to be rejected

Out of all the pain and suffering in humanity this by far must be one of the greatest. Its devastation is limitless. Rejection does not discriminate it will destroy the perfect relationship it will demolish the most successful human being. It has no substitute it seeks to dominate every human connection you have. Human rejection often leads to self-rejection. Self-rejection leads to self-destruction.

My brother and I were left with our grandparents who took good care of us. Many life changing events took place in our lives and our parents were absent. Because of this we were left Invalidated unprotected and open prey to the plan of the enemy. Our grandparents were pastors and preachers so everything we did revolved around church. We learned quickly that we were never going to get the attention that we so desperately needed, and we had become somewhat comfortable with it. But as time passed, we began to have our own fights and struggles in life that was fused by the rejection and absence of our parents. When you are denied attention from those that are responsible for your well-being it leaves a whole in your soul and you go through life trying to fill that void with anything that will bring you comfort peace and attention even if it's not for your wellbeing.

I was at a conference once and I heard a young man get up and say something so profound and relevant he said, "It's hard to stay committed and be stable in life after you've been rejected." When I heard those words, an alarm went off in me. It was what Oprah would call an, "Ah ha! moment." then and there life began to make sense to me. You see I had gone through most of my life being unable to complete and to commit to many important tasks and many times I wondered why. When you do not know how to handle rejection you create defense mechanisms and you began to do things to push people away unintentionally. I have messed up some great opportunities because I was trying to protect myself from false attacks. Rejection has the ability to put you in a fight that does not even exist. Many times, we hurt those that do not reject us and we find ourselves loyal to those that do. Because of the pain your parents put on you, you disrespect authority figures, because of the pain of your first marriage, your new spouse has become suspect in every way. Rejection creates an atmosphere of strife and if you do not deal with it you will become bitter and mean.

Those of us that have had maladjusted childhoods are often overwhelmed with the spirit of rejection. It is our greatest control point and if it is not dealt with properly it can become our greatest hinder. It will control our decision making in life. The greatest need of man is love and acceptance and when these two things are not fulfilled rejection is birthed. I cannot count the times I have been turned away and let down by those I really love. My biggest love language was giving because I felt like if I gave someone something, they would love me and want me around. But I was so wrong. Many took what I had and rejected my heart. I learned then, that just because they loved my gift does not mean they loved me.

I always wanted to be a part of something bigger than myself and fit in the crowd and be the life of the party without looking like a fool but that never happened for me. I was always the last one picked for the team. I remember playing hide and seek as a child in my neighborhood and when it was time for me to hide no one would look for me I was left lost and left only to wander back home alone. It had gotten so bad that I stayed inside the house and kept to myself in fear of being rejected I stayed away from family and friends. The absence of my parents left the biggest whole in my soul nothing could fill it. No one could brag on me enough tell me that they love me enough, no one could hold me or touch me enough. I constantly needed reassurance. I would enter relationships and do all I could to stay with that person even if they abused me, I would do anything for them if they did not leave me. I was so afraid of losing people I loved because all my childhood all the way up to my teenage years I lost people I loved and was rejected by those that I honored and admired.

I lived my life in an overwhelming depression and at the end of the day all I ever wanted was for someone to love me and it seemed as though I never got it. When I would reach out for love and acceptance, I was pushed away and told that I had to learn how to love myself. But how could I love someone that had never been loved? How could I embrace someone that did not know who they were because no one told him the truth about himself? I was fed lies by those that I loved and many of them said I was too black or too skinny or ugly or I acted too gay. I know those words that they spoke over me were not true but after hearing it at home, at school and among my peers at church I started to embrace what they said and what they saw so I accepted the lower level of life and did what I could do to dull that pain of rejection.

The sense of being unwanted hunted me for twenty-five years it was a deep wound that was hard to heal because it was put there by those that was to show me and introduce me to love and acceptance. You must understand that the spirit of rejection works hand and hand with the spirit of fear which can cause you to operate out of your emotions. I had to learn that rejection was the salt in life that gave me favor and flavor. Man's rejection is often God's protection. God did not want me to be like my father, so He had to get me away from him. God did not want me to practice a life of partying and clubbing, so he caused my mother to leave me in the company of her Holy Ghost filled parents. And the power of God that was on them got on me.

We cannot always avoid the pain of rejection but however we can decide to not allow it to control us and destroy the remainder of our lives. Whatever we didn't get as a child and whatever negative thing we received as a child; it is now time to let it all go. Embrace the fact that you were rejected. Had God wanted them to be in your life they would have stayed. Stop trying to make people be a part of your life that do not want you around. How long will you keep trying to convince people to stay with you? How long will you keep trying to talk people into loving you when they do not want you around you? Let them go! I do not care who they are. Stop lowering your value to be picked up by people that reject you. I do not care if it is a family member, if it is a friend you have had for twenty plus years, I do not care if it's a parent or a pastor. If they have shown you that they enjoy your absence more than they enjoy your presence let them embrace your truancy. Stop losing sleep over people that have forgotten you and ignored you. Read these words and read them out loud, YOU HAVE NOTHING TO PROVE TO

ANYONE THAT DOESN'T ADD VALUE TO YOUR LIFE! Stop crying about who left you and start embracing those who love you.

There are more people for you than there are against you, you just do not see it because you have minimized your world through the eyes of those that have rejected and abused you. Stop begging for attention from people that do not have your attention! Your purpose and destiny is not tied to people that rejected you. The very fact that they rejected you is a sure indication that you can make it without them. Rejection qualifies you for success for the great among us are those that were once unwanted unheard looked over and forgotten. You will never be good enough for them, you will never have enough for them, you will never do enough in their sight to make them accept you because you have been destined for greatness.

The truth is this, it is not that you're not good enough for them it's that they're not good enough for you. It is never our job to get people to love or to like us but it is our job to learn to love and accept ourselves. The power of self-love will be your dynamite in life that will cause you to explode and be successful in all that you do. The most rejected man that ever walked the face of this earth was the greatest man, that ever walked on the face of this earth and His name is Jesus. The scriptures declare that, "He is despised and rejected of men; a man of sorrows, and acquainted with grief: and we hid as it were our faces from him; he was despised, and we esteemed him not." (Isaiah 53:3 KJV) But Jesus did not allow it to change who He was. He was God rather they liked Him or not. Are you willing to be who you are even if they do not accept you? Are you willing to be great even when? You do not have their support? Nothing or nobody should ever have so much power over you that it stops you from being you. No one should ever have so much control over you that it paralyzes you to the point you cannot operate in your gifts and talents.

CHAPTER 3

THE COMPANY YOU KEEP

✦✦✦✦✦

"Be not deceived: evil communications corrupt good manners."

—1 Corinthians 15:33, King James Version

The people around you matter. If you want to know who people are, observe their surroundings. The friends they have defines the kind of person they are. You are who you hang out with. Your friends are a reflection of your future. My grandmother would say it like this, "birds of a feather flock together. "You have to get to a place in your life where you set a standard for yourself. Its time out for settling and taking things that you don't have to take. There are certain things you just should not permit, and negative people should be one of them. Every time you expose yourself to negative people you open yourself up to failure. Most of the time we tolerate things that are not good for us because we have been motivated by fear. Scared of what people will say or think of us if we pulled away. Scared of being alone and friendless.

The most difficult act of courage that you could ever perform is to lose yourself from the people you have grown familiar with. Often times we keep company with people that don't challenge us. If you are the smartest among the group of people you keep company with then you will never grow or be better at what you do. You should at least have two individuals in your life that jerks the slack out of you, individuals that are smarter than you and will not allow you to get by with sloping living. Every time you act out of character or do something stupid, they are right there to call you out on it. People like this fall under the **Faithful Father** category.

Being a father of five beautiful children is one of the greatest things that has ever happened to me. There is nothing my children could ever do or ever be to make me stop loving them. It is my job to love them through it and to love them to it. As a father I am always doing all I can to push them to be greater and better than me. Whenever I give them instructions to do something it is not the task at hand that I'm concerned about it's the overall picture. I realize if they can learn to obey me, they won't have trouble obeying those that are in authority. If I teach them to work now when they grow older it will be second nature to them to have a job and work hard for what they want. Faithful fathers push you into the greater you and celebrate you once you get there. They are your coach in life, cheering you on while chastening you at the same time.

The people that you have in your life right now should be reducing your stress, not causing it. You should be with people that make you feel good about you being you and they should always challenge you to be a better you if they are not doing these things, they fall under the **Following Fan** category. Fans are people that follow you because of what you have and what you can do for them. They do not want you to change they want you to remain the same for their benefit. Your close company should be people that celebrate you they should be the people that push you to the top does not pull you down. When you have obtained and achieved all of your goals in life they shouldn't be mad at you or jealous.

You can't be friends with individuals that hate your success. These people fall under the **Fake Family** category. Most of your family members want to see you succeed but they do not want you to do it without them. It is strange but true. Your family will celebrate you as long as you are giving them some of the success that you worked hard for. These blood relatives are leeches they suck you dry and when you run out because you gave to them, they will abandon you. So, beware of the fake family. I have learned that many times the company that we need to walk away from are people we really love, and those people are most of the time family members. I often say that, "the people you love the most can be the ones that will hurt you the most."

Being bullied and taunted did not start at school or in some foreign place for me, I was mistreated and talked about right at home. As a toddler my mom kept me up under her. I went everywhere with her she would not let me leave her sight. Until I was about five years old, I was stuck up under my mother and when I was not with her, I was with my grandmother. I was so close to my grandmother I use to comb her hair cook her food even help her pick out her clothes for church on Sundays. So, after being under them so much I took on their mannerisms. I would roll my eyes talk with my hands sit with my legs crossed just like they did. And because I was exposed to their behaviors I was talked about and mistreated and called names.

I remember hearing someone talk about me after a church service one night. They said, "that boy know he act like a little girl; I believe he has that gay spirit on him." I was only eleven years old at the time. I did not know what being gay was all about, but I assumed it was something awfully bad. Conversations and accusations went on like that about me for years. Every time I would hear talk like that it would break my heart because I really loved people. Anytime you have to prove something to somebody in order to keep them in your life, you do not need them. Please understand what I am saying, friends are not bad family members are not bad having fans is not a bad thing but knowing the difference and knowing their motives is the important thing. You know a person's motives based upon how they act when you are down to your last or when you are up to your greatest. If you have people around you that are not sensitive to your future, cut them off. Go through your friends list and start purging it. I know it is hard to let go of people that you have a rich history with but if that friendship is not pushing you to greatness than that friendship is in vain.

I know how hard it can start over a new life without the people you once believed in and supported. I have never really been that person that liked to cut people off or take joy in blocking and deleting people out of my life. Every person I have had to let go or walk away from it was very hard for me. It took some time for me to really get to a place of normalcy after I have had to release them. To be very honest with you I was horrible at choosing the right friends and the right company to hang around. Because I was abused and abandoned as a child, I never thought very highly of myself so I hung out with people that abused and bullied me. Please understand this, that you choose your friends based upon how you see or view yourself. If you see yourself as a loser your friends will be losers, if you see yourself as nothing then you will keep company with a bunch of useless nobodies. Look at where you are right now, you are where you are because you chose a friend that connected you to that position. Become intentional about who you connect yourself with. Stop going through life collecting people just to have a large following. If you want to be effective you have to hang out with effective people. Find a coach and a mentor that will influence your life for the better. I know it feels good to be the best in the room. I know you like to stand out in the crowd and be known as the hardest worker or the smartest intellectual or the most significant. But if you are always the best in the room you have no room to grow. And if you are not growing, you are dying. If you do not surround yourself with people that are better than you your dreams, your visions and your business will become stagnant and eventually die. Hang with the best and you will become the best. Winning is contagious. It is like a virus, once you expose yourself to it, it will get a hold of you and change your life forever. Expose yourself to winners and watch what happens to you. Stop compromising your life for people that do not care if you succeed or fail. Step out of your comfort zone and level up. The only way to do that is to change your surroundings. Who you want to be and who you want to become is predicated upon who you allow yourself to be vulnerable with. When my wife and I first started dating, people used to think we were brother and sister. They used to say you all look alike. And in the beginning, I did not get it and I did not see it but as time went on, I realized why people thought that. It was simply because her and I were always together, and we began to pick up on each other's ways and habits. We shared the same language and the same movements. We are rubbing off on one another. You see who you hang with imparts in you. Whatever they do you do; however, they act, you act. So, what is it going to be? Will you change your company? Will you continue to be content with the life you have with others? Will you lose the familiar and grabs hold to the extraordinary life God has for you? Your next great promotion in life is predicated upon the company you keep and the connections you make. Please know that if you are to walk into a better life, you are going to have to have the courage to leave the crowd, dedication requires separation.

CHAPTER 4

THE POWER OF PRAYER AND MEDITATION

◆◆◆◆◆◆◆

"And he spake a parable unto them to this

end, that men ought always to pray,

and not to faint;"

—Luke 18:1, King James Version

There will always be questions you do not have answers to there will always be problems that you may not be able to solve, situations that will go beyond your control. But in all that you must be sure of this one thing and that is this, you were put here on this earth for a purpose and you have been designed and created by a God that longs to communion with you and share time and space and eternity with you. You did not make yourself, you did not emerge or materialize out of thin air. But you were manufactured by God in the Heavens. He knew your name before your parents thought of your name. "Listen, O isles, unto me; and hearken, ye people, from far; The LORD hath called me from the womb; from the bowels of my mother hath he made mention of my name." (Isaiah 49:1, KJV). He formed you while you were growing inside of your mother and set you apart to be His and to do His will. "Before I formed thee in the belly I knew thee; and before thou camest forth out of the womb I sanctified thee, and I ordained thee a prophet unto the nations." (Jeremiah 1:5, KJV) You are not a mistake you are not a worthless nothing on this earth without a purpose but you are a human being made in the image and likeness of God. When you subjugate your thoughts to understand this you will get the revelation of who you are and why you are here. Never allow the world around you to overtake your spiritual awareness within you because it can, and it will. What's around you is temporal but what's in you is eternal. "While we look not at the things which are seen, but at the things which are not seen: for the things which are seen are temporal; but the things which are not seen are eternal."(2nd Corinthians 4:18, KJV) Allow what is in you to become commodious and avowed so that all will see and know that you are bigger and brighter than your darkest ugliest weakness and you do this by tapping into the power of God through prayer.

Waking up in the middle of the night I could hear the sounds of crying, weeping and wailing in the other room. The sound did not carry a grieving or depressed milieu but that of liberation and ravishment. It was the sound of my grandmother and grandfather praying. I would often peek into their room slightly cracking the door my little four year old eyes would behold the most beautiful thing in the world. He would be on one end of the bed on his knees and she would be on the

28

other side of the bed on her knees and they both would be crying out calling on the name of Jesus. Seeing this sparked a fire in me. I wanted to know this Jesus they were crying out to. Often my grandmother would go off in tongues and the power of God would be on her so heavy she would quicken. I would hear her say, "Save my children Lord, you know their heart Jesus give them a do right mind Lord, most of all Lord look on me." She would go on until she would get up off her knees and paste the floor praising and worshiping God. This was how I was introduced to Jesus Christ. Two country Pentecostal pastors from South Georgia who so happens to be my grandparents unveiled to me the life of Christendom. They did not just tell me about Jesus they showed me Jesus. Watching and listening to these dynamic people pray preach and meditate on the word of God changed my life. They kept my brother and I in church almost every day of the week and all day on Sunday. I embraced this life style right away. There was always something in me that caused me to gravitate towards God. In my early years I saw my grandparents and other saints in the faith have many spiritual encounters with God and if I would tell you some of them you would not believe me. But it was not until I was eleven years old that I had my own personal spiritual encounter with God.

My Grandparents were pastors of this small country church down in Forsyth Georgia The church was so small it did not even have an indoor bathroom at the time. It set back in the woods without a foundation held up by bricks and plywood but the power of God was ever present in that place. It was the summer of 1993 the church was in revival It was to be a three-night revival but the revival ended up lasting eight days. In the Pentecostal church we would have what you call a tarrying service where many would gather around the altar on their knees and call on the name of Jesus until they are filled with the Holy Ghost with the evidence of speaking in tongues according to Acts 2:1-4. Every night of that revival I would go to the altar crying and calling on Jesus. For many days I did this. On the seventh night of the revival I was at my seat in the back of the church during what we would call devotional service. The saints were singing and in high praise. At that moment I prayed to God and under my breath I said, "God fill me with your Spirit I want to feel you for real." After speaking these words I stood to my feet clapping my hands joining in with the saints in praise and something like heat hit me in the face and I raised my hands to say hallelujah but something happen to me in that moment and I began to speak in other tongues crying uncontrollably leaping shouting and dancing under this God spell that had come upon me. I cannot explain the joy and the peace I felt in that moment all I know is that I had entered a place that was not of this world overtaken by a presence that was not of this world this was my personal encounter with God and from that day until now my life has never been the same I was only eleven years old.

It is my testimony that my connection with God has kept me through great danger great abuse and horrific events in my life. God did not cause these things in my life but He kept me through them and used them to keep me connected to Him. Out of every tragic and misadventure in my life prayer was birthed giving me the ability to subjoin to the creator of this world in whom I believe and know is Jesus Christ.

What is prayer?

Prayer is not you using God like some genie in a bottle or a Santa Claus for you to get what you want. Prayer is not sending God to run your errands. Prayer is not getting God to do your will, prayer is getting you prepared to do God's will. Prayer is the portal to the heavens that reaches God giving you the ability to release the supernatural power of God in your life. To show you what eyes have not seen, allowing you to hear what ears have not heard, giving you ideas that have not entered into the hearts of men. "But as it is written, Eye hath not seen, nor ear heard, neither have entered into the heart of man, the things which God hath prepared for them that love him." (1st Corinthians 2:9, KJV). Many intellectuals believe that God in Heaven is far removed and is far away but I write to you my beloved to straighten that lie out. God is not far away and He is not far removed but God is as close as your next prayer. Prayer does not need proof it needs practice. It is the light in a dark world. Prayer is the ultimate prerogative that awakens the spirit man within you. If your life is void of this implementation you are impuissant in this tenebrous world. From the beginning of time it has been the will of the almighty to have a connection with us and prayer gives us that connection. Every great man and every great woman did not become great until they connected with a higher call that higher call being prayer. Prayer is that tool in which you use to beat back the hand of the enemy it is the small flame that sets your world on fire. Without this you are left dry destitute and alone. Prayer causes the universe to yield and to bow at your command (Joshua 10:12) Prayer will cause God to change His mind (Exodus 32:9-14). Prayer will cause a barren woman to become pregnant and give birth (1st Samuel 1:4-28). Prayer opens doors that cannot be shut (Colossians 4:3) Prayer is the medicine that will cure a troubled mind of anxiety (Philippians 4:6&7) Prayer helps us in our weakness and condemn our infirmities in the presence of the almighty God (Romans 8:26-27) Prayer will enlarge your territory, keep you from harm and rid you from pain (1st Chronicles 4:10) Prayer will heal the land (2nd Chronicles 7:14) Prayer saves the sick and raises you up and if you have committed sins you shall be forgiven (James 5:15&16) The most powerful apparatus given to any Christian or saint of the most high God is the ability to pray. Once you tap into this propensity there is no stopping you, the impossibilities in your life becomes possible.

When do I pray?

Many times prayer has been used in time of extremity when it should be used unremittingly. It should not be your 911 call to God but it should be your 411 to Him, allowing Him to show you who He is and revealing to you who you are. Stop waiting for things to fall apart in your life before you pray. Pray before things fall apart. Prayer in good times will give you the vehemence in life when bad times come suddenly upon you. *At all times:* Psalms 34:1 I will bless the Lord at all times: His praises shall continually be in my mouth. Prayer in not for the lazy. It takes work patience and consistency. I have noticed in this day and age that many want to be perfect without practice. It is the enactment of prayer that causes things to happen. You can't give up and stop praying just because the answer isn't coming fast enough or coming like you want it to. You have to errorless in the practice of prayer if you want to see results. The inspired scripture of this chapter Luke 18:1 shows you that if you don't always pray you will faint. If you faint you give up, you cave in and you quit. Those that quit are individuals that refused to pray. Prayer should be the river in you that flows without stopping. Having consistent communication with God gives you favor and instant access in the heavenly realm. Ephesians 6:18 and pray in the Spirit on all occasions. with all kinds of prayers and requests. With this in mind, be alert and always keep on praying for all the saints. 1st. Thessalonians 5:17 the Apostle Paul tells us to pray continually. Simply meaning having an unstoppable viable relationship with God. This will put you on the Road of perfection. I am grateful for my humble Pentecostal upbringing. It is in this upbringing that I learned who God was who God is and who He can be in my life. Keeping an open line into the spirit world through Christ Jesus will allow you to operate in absolute power. When your will and emotions yields and serves the spirit man with in you who is Christ Jesus my friend that's when you have mastered to operate in absolute power. It is prayer and meditation on Him that gives you that ability. Never abandon the posture of prayer. This is your secret portion that causes your world to spin in control.

In The Morning

Please know and understand that each day you wake up is a reminder that God is not finished with you and you have entered into a day of newness. Each day you wake up is a gift for you to start over. The most important part of your day is the morning. It is said that the most important meal of the day is breakfast for it is the meal that fuels you and prepares you for the day. But I want to challenge you, before you put anything in your mouth let prayer and praise proceed out of your mouth. Prayer sets the course of your day quicker than any meal. In Job 38:12 God asks Job, "Hast thou commanded the morning since thy days; and caused the dayspring to know his place"? When you open your mouth in the spirit of thanksgiving and gratitude and speak to God in the morning He will set your day in order and cause it to work for you without you working for it. Before you allow your day to pollute you with its issues and cares began to cast your cares on God the minute you open your eyes and it will empower you for your purpose that day. For the past couple of years I have made it a habit to call on God and tap into the power within early in the morning. I can testify to you and tell you that practicing this works. I'm not a morning person but I had to fight through my feelings and my wants to channel the light within me which is God. This doesn't mean that I haven't had bad days but this does mean that I have had the help of God in those days. It gave God permission to handle my business. When you open your mouth to pray in the morning you free the hand of God and you unchain the gifts of God in you. Morning meditation gives you a head start on your day, picking you up before you fall. This gives you daily positive expectations. (Psalm 5:3) Positive expectation puts you in miracle territory.

How do I pray?

After receiving Christ at an early age of eleven I had no outline or format on how to pray and receiving answers from God. Although I saw what my grandparents did I didn't know how to put in into practice for myself so I just did what I saw them do and it worked for a while. I learned that me getting on my knees shouting and hollering was not going to give me the answers I really needed in life I had to learn how to channel my spirit and find that connection with God and speak to Him clearly and be specific about what I wanted from Him. Let me show you what I came up with that works for me and I pray it works for you. This layout is like a culvert for me and how I get to my God place.

-**I**solate

-**P**raise

-**R**estore

-**A**sk

-**Y**ield

*I*solate

Before you enter into that place of prayer posture make sure you find a place around you were you can be completely alone. Many of us do not like to be by ourselves or separated from others because it makes us feel vulnerable and disconnected from the world. But it's those very feelings that causes your connection with God to be intensified. When you are Isolated you are free from distractions and negative outside influences. It is important that you have a place for yourself a time, place and space that you do not share with others but it's just you and God. Isolation can cause a great calm and quiets your inner man from the cares and voices of your yesterday and yesteryears. When I first started praying I use to run to the back bathroom of our house. It was a place where I knew I would not be disturbed. I would call on the name of the Lord so until when others would come to use the bathroom after I prayed they would feel the energy and the force of God in that small space. I would get on my knees next to the toilet and seek God. this may be funny to you but this was the only place I knew no one would come and try and find me. It was my secret place that I shared with God and myself. Find you a secret place it is so important. Your geographic location in prayer should be a consecrated area dedicated to that which is clean and holy. Jesus even tells us that, "when you pray go into your secret closet and close the door and pray to your Father, who is unseen. Then your Father who sees what is done in secret will reward you." (Matthew 6:6) So find your secret place an inaudible place and shutdown. When you enter that place don't say anything for about five to ten minutes Just calm your soul and listen to the silence around you and clear your spirit of all noise and your mind of all craziness. Close your eyes breath deeply and embrace the silence. Remember Psalm 91:1, "He that dwelleth in the *secret place* of the most High shall abide under the shadow of the Almighty"

*P*raise

After your spirit is calm and you have isolated yourself began to tap into the power of God within you. You do that by opening up your mouth praising and thanking God for all He has done. Begin to tell Him who He is and what He is to you by doing this you are inviting Him into your area and into your being even more. Praise is the highest demonstration of your faith. A faith that is not demonstrated is a faith that can not be trusted. Please know that true praise can not be practiced or done in the mind it has to be vocal. Thinking about praise is not advantageous. You must part your lips open your mouth and say something. Shout joyfully unto the Lord (Psalm 98:4) Doing this also reminds you who God is and who you are it puts you in a place of humility. Humility is the power that every great successful human being promenade in. And in this God is pleased and your soul is free from all fear. Praise is the usher that leads God to the throne of your heart. Stop what you are doing right now and begin to part your lips and tell God who He is to you tell Him how much you love Him and need Him and the power within you will begin to commence and blaze up like a fire. Do it now.

Restore

This is when you start repenting and disclose all of your faults failures and sins to God. Asking Him to make you new again and refresh you. This will restore your relationship with Him and free you from all guilt shame and condemnation. Please know that if you have anything in your heart that is not true to you or God it will cause your connection with God to be distorted. Psalm 66:18 *If I regard iniquity in my heart, the Lord will not hear me:* Going into prayer without acknowledging your sin is like cooking and preparing a great meal without washing your hands after you've used the bathroom. Always be true to who you are taking that in prayer before God who will purify you from all unrighteousness. (1st John 1:9) Never talk to God without clearing the air with Him. Make it right with Him and He will make it right for you. You are never too big that you can't recognize your faults and failures and repent of them. By doing this it rids you of self loathing and inner fears which can hold you back from operating in the spirit of excellence. Restoring your walk with God during this time pushes the refresh button on your life making things new again, giving you clean air to breath.

*A*sk

Don't be afraid to ask God for what you want. He longs to take care of you and provide for you but He needs your permission to move. He will never violate your will or force Himself upon you He wants you to ask Him and come to Him as a child coming to a mother wanting to be nurtured. We often times bypass all other things and come straight to this point of asking but when you build a relationship with this amazing God and ask Him boldly for what you want the answers and blessings hit a little different. Getting what you want from someone who you do not know can be a good thing but receiving something that you want from a person you have a relationship is far greater. Jesus says, "if you abide in me and my words abide in you, you can ask for whatever you want and it shall be given to you (St. John 7:7) Being in God and His word and His ways sealed in you gives you guaranteed access to the throne room of Heaven to ask God for what you want. Many times as Christians we go lacking because we fail to ask God for help and sometimes what we ask God for is too small. Please know that the God we serve is the God of the impossibilities He can do anything but fail. So go ahead step out on your faith and ask Him for the impossible and watch Him do it! If you have faith enough to ask Him He has the power to do it! You have not because you ask not (James 4:3) So stop getting angry with God because He hasn't given you what you want or what you need when you haven't asked Him for it. Be careful for nothing: but in everything by prayer and supplication with thanksgiving let your requests be made known unto God. (Philippians 4:6).

*Y*ield

Surrendering it all to God and allowing Him to take complete control brings you into a place of peace. End your prayer by letting God know that you belong to Him and that He has your permission to do whatever He wants. Never leave prayer without giving God an opportunity to move or to speak back to you. Remember prayer is communication with God and communication is when both parties are speaking and listening to one another. Never do all the talking in prayer leave room for God to speak impart and reveal His presence. End your prayer like you started surrender to God get quiet and listen to what He has to say. His voice may not sound like thunder or a big audible sound but it may be that peace within you pulling you into a specific direction. Never tell God what you want without listening to what He wants.

Conclusion

You have been made and created by that which is all life and all light (St. John 1:4) by giving yourself over to that daily makes you vulnerable to the power of great success. Being known by many does not define success. Stop trying to be known by many people and know who you are and be known by the greater power in you which is God. The only way to know His power is to pray. Nothing happens less we pray. You should build an altar everywhere you go. For it is at the altar where your weaknesses and failures are burned and destroyed and your strengths and your merits are revealed.

CHAPTER 5

FORGIVENESS, YOUR WINGS TO THE TOP

For he that hath, to him shall be given: and he that hath not, from him shall be taken even that which he hath.

—Mark 4:25, King James Version

It was only two years after my great God encounter that I was sexually molested and abused. A man that became a drug addict and an alcoholic a man who lost his way so bad in life that he became a pedophile molesting three of his own children one of his step-daughters and other nieces and nephews. He dumped his dysfunction on me the minute he decided to violate me sexually. I grew so angry and bitter with him and with those who knew the truth and encouraged me to hide it, I often times thought of killing him and killing myself. The feelings of hopelessness and worthlessness would overtake me until I cried uncontrollably, I would fight and fly off the handle I was quick tempered and violent. The horrific act that had engulfed me weighed on me like tombstones on a grave plot until I became dead on the inside.

After escaping the abuse and moving in with my grandparents, my molester tracked me down and came to my grandparents' house and talked to them alone saying that I had made sexual moves on him and that I tried to perform oral sex on him and that is why I was running. This lie he concocted because he was afraid that I was going to tell the truth about his disgusting acts he had performed on me. But I did not and I was too afraid and too ashamed to disclose any information like that. Please understand and know that I was only fourteen years old at the time, all I wanted was to be accepted and to be a child. I was stripped of those things and left to deal with my torn heart and broken emotions. I hated him. He had destroyed my childhood and now here he is sitting in my grandparents' living room with his legs crossed and my mother at his side destroying my fourteen-year character, how evil can you be? I was left without a voice no way of defending myself and no one came to see about me or to believe me. It was at that moment I knew that if I was to live I had to do two things, number one pour myself in God and His church and number two, take care of myself both of these tasks became very difficult as the years went by and I got older. I hated so many people and despised so many of those that abused me and tried to bring me down. Most of all I hated myself and I just did not want to live anymore. I hated me because I felt like I allowed this to happen to me. I loathed myself because of the struggle I had with my identity and I couldn't love my wife the way she wanted me to love her and the way she deserved to be loved. I was so broken and dysfunctional I thought love was sex and sex was love. I opened myself up to people that meant me no good I connected to those that abused me like he did. On top of all of this I was preaching and singing everywhere broken and shattered. I had no sense of direction no hope on the inside. I loved to preach and sing because that was the only time I got positive attention and the only time I really felt like I was loved. Ministry was filling the void of love and acceptance in my life temporarily. When ministry stopped and I had to dissolve my church it left me depressed. Years had passed and I was now a full grown man with five children and a wife and a flourishing ministry which was now dissolved and abandoned. I found myself in a mental institute, diagnosed with chronic depression this man of God was found on the side of the road trying to kill Himself.

How did I get here? How did all of this happen to me? This is not how I planned my life this is not how it was supposed to be. The whole world had turned on me and I seemed to be hated by many and abandoned by those I wanted in my life. I was admitted into a mental hospital for seven days and it was on the third day that I realized why life is not working for me. This is the part of my life I would like to call, *"Flying without Wings"* If you are to vanquish your past, mastering the art of forgiveness and handling offences well is essential. We live in a world where we put more energy into holding on than we do letting go. Let me make this clear, your strength is not predicated upon what you have held onto but it is defined by what you had to walk away from and let go of. The road of success will cost you everything. You lose your way to the top. Tripping up, falling, and failing is a part of the journey. Accept that fact but never I mean never embrace it as a lifestyle. Failure is to be an event in your life, not an identity. You make it an identity when you embrace your fears and receive life lower than what your dreams are. Flying is never a comfort companion in the beginning, but an enemy to your will and emotions. It will challenge every part of you and everything that is connected to you. Your first stage of flying will cause pain to your spirit of ease and comfort destroying your mindset of just walking but yet developing your will to soar above the things that are not connected to your destination and your purpose in life. After being abused sexually, mentally, emotionally, and spiritually for years, I was angry with the world. Many times I felt like I had nothing to hold on to but anger it was my only comfort in life. I confronted everything and everybody that crossed me. I became reckless and fearless of God and man. I did not know the root cause of this was me being unable to forgive those that hurt me. I did not know how to forgive them all I knew was that I was done wrong and someone needed to pay. I was given a debt that I did not owe and could not pay. Someone had to pay and it wasn't going to be me. I became stuck. I was stuck in the thickness of the mud of revenge. I had made up my mind that every one that ever wronged me was going to pay one way or another. I wished death upon the man that molested me. He had to die even if it was by my hands. "How dare you live and you take life, how dare you live, and you hurt others. It is not fair, ``I thought to myself. I'm suffering from the pain you placed on me while you rejoice and smile living the good life after you done your evil to me. I carried this muddy footprint of revenge and tracked it everywhere I went. I did not see good in anyone. Even those that were close to me I grew to dislike them because I saw something in them that I saw in the ones that caused me pain. And because there are no perfect people I only saw their dysfunctions because all life ever gave me was dysfunctional moments. And what you see is what you will obtain. My muddy footprint was on every part of my marriage and it tracked heavily in my ministry. I left dirt everywhere I went. I did not know how to rid myself of this mud I did not know how to walk and run without sliding through the dirt that life had given me. Flying was a foreign ability to me, the very thought of having wings was a myth. I felt like you had to come from a rich functional family to go high in life. No good thing will come to people like me. I'm a poor skinny black dark skin flamboyant man in America and I'm super loud. All the odds was against me I thought to myself. Not knowing that I was qualified to be great the only thing that disqualified me was the mud of revenge and forgiveness that was underneath my feet. I had to learn to fly. Forgiveness are the wings of the overcomers. If you want to become a great an awesome individual you are going to have to learn to clear the runway in your mind and rid yourself of things that weigh on you and pull you down so you can fly. I remember the great moments and events in my life that were short lived. And I would always ask God, "Why can't I seem to get off the ground, why every time I try and make a step forward

I am pushed twenty steps back, why can't I soar like the others?" It was simply because I did not have wings. I had muddy nasty feet soaked in revenge and unforgiveness. In order for me to mount up and be free and clean from the pain of my past I had to learn to master the art of forgiveness. And I did not want to. I could not move I could not think of life beyond the pain that was forced upon me. So I suffered with mental illness. I grew depressed each day that went by I was so overwhelmingly sad I forgot what happiness felt like. I was so concerned about how I was so brutally violated. I was so overwhelmed with the thought of how I was rejected how I was looked down on and forgotten and passed by and how alone I was I had no room for nothing in my life but the pain bestowed upon me. So I held on to it like darkness holding on to night. And like night time my soul grew darker and darker as the years grew by. So dark that I could not do anything without hurting someone. When I preached I preached man. Judging and hollering and condemning people to Hell. I had no mercy on anyone and why should I when no one had mercy on me? I was mean to my wife I yelled and screamed at her when I did not get my way. I would throw fits if she tried to come at me wrong, I chasten my kids angrily and abusive. Doing to them what was done to me not realizing I was casting the shadow of darkness upon them that was laid upon me. I want you to understand that when you hold on to pain it doesn't just affect you, it affects everyone around you, especially the people you love and the people that love you. Your pain carries a weight and your not the only one carrying it, everyone you involve yourself with on a day to day bases carry it each time you exercise your authority. I remember being in the mental hospital and I was crying and sobbing and I told God, "I can't do this anymore, I hate my life I hate what happen to me. Why did you let this happen to me why didn't you stop this why did you call me to preach and sing, why did you give me a beautiful wife and five children and allow me to have so much pain in my life? God it's not fair what they did to me it's just not right!" For hours I yelled and complained to God shaking my fist up in the air towards Him as if He was my enemy. I groaned with a mad voice as I cried out to God on that night. Holding on to all that anger and bitterness I realized at that moment that I was not just mad at my violators and myself I was mad and angry with God. The voice of God returned to me in that hour, sitting in that padded room, alone and broken. God spoke to me in a whisper of a voice and said to me, "Why are you so heavy?" Why have you allowed this to overtake you? Don't you know that I am your God and I am in you and I will never put you in something that I will not bring you out of? Let go of what they did to you, remember that you yourself are not perfect you have broken many hearts and disappointed many individuals including me, wouldn't you like for Me along with them to forgive you and restore you?" I replied to God, "I don't care "You lie" He answered, "do not deceive yourself everyone wants to be forgiven, everyone wants to be shown mercy and love. You don't just want it you need it." At that moment I wept bitterly before the presence of God and I cried and I cried, about things that I never took the time to cry about. I grieved the death of my grandmother for the first time I was so angry with her for dying so suddenly and so young. I was mad at her for not being alive and seeing me through my rough times like she always did. I was bitter towards her because she died without giving me a chance to prove to her how special and how great I was. I wanted her to know that I graduated high school and was going to college I wanted her to see my beautiful wife and play with my five amazing children. I was so mad and yet so hurt that she left me to deal with all the foolishness the family and the church had gotten itself into because she was gone. I purged and cried for an hour over her transition and the death of her ministry. I wondered why she didn't leave me in charge what was so wrong with me that I couldn't help lead her church. She died without leaving anyone the mantel. It all went to the grave and into the hands of those that did not know her vision nor did they know her as an individual. I cried until my eyes were swollen as if I had been in a fight and lost. I wept and cried. I wept over the passing of my grandfather who had died only two years before. I cried over him like a baby crying for the next sip of milk after the bottle had been empty. So had my life had been since he was no longer in it. He was the first true male figure in my life. The first man to show me love and tell me he loves me. The bottle of my soul was empty and *wanted more of what he had to offer me. I* did not want him to leave me. He saw the greatness in me when others laughed and mocked me. I reached out into the air with my hands lifted as I cried and grieved his death wishing he were there to embrace me. I continued to sob over the absence and rejection of my father I cried and I cried and I cried. I cursed and used profane language when I wept and grieved over the child that was molested at thirteen I uttered out words of hate and pain as I called out the name of my molester. The tears flowed down my cheek dripping off my beard as I cried over the pain that the pastors and bishops had placed upon me when I served their church. For three days, I cried, I cried, I cried, and I cried some more. I was told so many times not to cry and that real men do not cry. I was beaten as a child and after I was beat I was told to shut up and stop all that crying I fell off my bike and hurt my knees really bad and I was told that I was a little punk for crying like that and I needed to grow up. I'll never forget when I saw my grandfather lying in bed after he had passed away I became so overwhelmed with sorrow and hurt I passed out in the middle of the hospice floor screaming and crying and someone came up to me and said, "stand up be a man stop all that." And because I suppress my pain it left me angry resentful and in a mental institute. Not showing emotions drove me crazy. The painful thoughts that haunted me for years grew fervent in my thoughts until my brain boiled and cooked my emotions and left me done. Something I thought I had gotten over and moved away from but I realized that just because you don't address and issue doesn't mean the issue will disappear. You must deal with it one way or another. Your life was made to handle even the most painful places. So I say to you cry my brothers cry my sisters let the tears flow.

There is healing in your tears release them and allow them to wash your heart and you will find the weight in life gets lighter and your ability to forgive and let go of the past and the pain will form. Do not ignore your pain don't suppress your feelings deal with them before they deal with you.

The worst thing my religion ever taught me was how to be fake. Religion taught me how to lie. Teaching me to ignore my feelings and just move on. For years I practiced this wicked terrible sect and it had profit me nothing. "Just move on", they said. "Ignore how you feel and grab a hold to your faith and believe God." I went to church dancing shouting and singing doing all the things that religion taught me but it never taught me I mean never taught me how to deal with the reality of how to live life. And out of ignorance I kept practicing this religious exercises Sunday after Sunday day after day. Driving myself down a dead end road of destruction. I was functioning in the church but dysfunctional at home. I was so out of order I did not know how to breathe right unless the church told me. I gave myself over to something that did not give itself over to me because when I had reached my deadened road they were nowhere to be found. All the false teaching and manipulative acts came to light and left me bitter and broken. Telling me to believe God while stabbing me is not mentorship, telling me to have faith in what God says while gossiping about me is not leading, its abuse. It was all abuse and a type of bullying. Being open rebuked in front of my family, my friends and loved ones was not constructive criticism it was persecution from the pulpit. These are the reality of the church today and the face of religion I have had to deal with from day to day. How can I believe God when I am broken and shattered? How can I believe God when I'm so miserable and my constant thoughts are death. The thoughts of death would visit me in the morning with a cup of coffee, hopelessness and doubt. But no one knew this because we all saw life through our eyes of religion and not the eyes of reality. Reality was kicking our behind while religion was slowly killing us through the ignorance of our corrupt maladjusted theology. Years had passed and I was going nowhere fast. I had allowed myself to be faithful to abuse and abuse became a strong companion and a poisonous provider to my soul.

Oh how I had to let go of the hurt that the local church had placed on me and put me through. I never knew people of God could be so evil and mean. The pain of church hurt carries different weight because of expectations of godly people are held to a higher standard. We fail to realize that they are people as well. All that hurt and pain, I had to grow from it and learn to fly. I didn't see myself as big or as of any importance in this life because of how I was treated but the minute I saw my significance in this world I knew that I had to let go of all the foolishness that was taught to me and forgive those that were the professors of foolish faith and deadly doctrine. You are too big to allow others who are not present to control you. Why do you give power to people that hold no real significance to your future? Why do you allow yourself to be angry with those that are hurting themselves. Please know that what they did to you wasn't right and how they treated you wasn't right but they didn't know it was you. They did not know who you really were they did not see you they saw only what the enemy showed them. They did not know. They were fools. And we ignore fools for their ability to comprehend and understand is absent. On the cross Jesus shouted out, "Father forgive them, for they know not what they do. (Luke 23:34) Christ refused to go to the grave angry and mad at people that did not know who He was. I challenge you now let it go. Do not go to the grave mad and bitter at those that do not know or didn't know who you were because had they known they would had never involved themselves with you in that way. I want you to stop reading this book for a moment and go somewhere by yourself and began to talk to God and began to tell Him that you let go of everyone who wronged you tell Him what they did how they did it tell Him how unfair it was tell Him how angry you are about it and release it and free the person of that debt and free yourself of that weight and fly.

For some of you that have been really hurt and the pain has grown so deep you can't let go, for you forgiveness may be a journey and not a destination you may have to grow into it instead of going into it. But however, you do it just make sure you find yourself flying. I heard the late Billy Graham once say, "When one finds himself in a place where it seems like he cannot forgive his brethren, when he prays and as God for forgiveness of his sins, he should pray for the brethren that he cannot forgive."

EVOLVE

My beloved brothers and sisters love yourself. Love yourself enough to let go of all the unjust things that ever happened to you. You deserve to fly. Out of all the things you have had to crawl through walk through and run through, it is time to take flight. And once you finally mount up you will see that things are smaller than they appear to be when you are not so close to them. Fly until you see things growing smaller, fly until your ears pop and you can no longer hear the foolish opinions of others, fly until you are able to rise above every storm that will come in your life. Go higher and higher until others must look up and see you your life will be a testimony and an inspiration that they too can fly. And when they ask you, "How did you get so high?" Your response will be "I let it all go.

CHAPTER 6

THOU SHALL NOT FEAR

+ + ◆ ◆ ◆ + +

For God hath not given us the spirit of fear; but of

power, and of love, and of a sound mind.

-2 Timothy 1:7, King James Version

It was the fall of 1986 when my grandfather had his nervous breakdown. My grandmother and I along with my brother were in the back yard hanging the laundry on the clothesline. The wind was slightly blowing the orange and brown leaves of that old oak tree was gently falling to the ground like snowflakes. My grandmothers white dress blew in the wind as she pends the sheets and the shams to the clothes line. The air was fresh and refreshing unlike the mind and soul of my grandfather. He approached us with this crazy look in his eyes saying that he had been with God and that he was a prophet. "I'm a prophet sent from God!" He shouted waving a long fishing rod in his left hand. "I'm a true man of God and nobody believes me, but I'm about to show you, everybody is gone know and they gone see that Grandfather Weems is real!" Now there was a lake that stood about a thousand feet from our backyard. This lake stretched out about two to three miles going through the backside of the town of South Georgia. Many people would come from across the local county to fish therein. My grandfather looked at my grandmother in the face holding tightly to that fishing rod with his eyes dancing around in his head he said, "I'm going to part the water." She looked at him and laughed, holding the end of a sheet in her hand and a clothespin in the other. "Grandfather what in the world are you talking about, you can't part that water." Laughing in disbelief shaking her head she glanced over at my brother and I as she reached to get the clothes basket she said, "come on y'all lets go in the house grandfather done loss his mind." When my grandfather heard that he shouted the more his face turned solid red eyes wide he said to us, "yall watch this." He stormed off headed in the direction of the lake as we went in the house. Dropping the clothes basket on the kitchen floor my grandmother stood at the sink looking out the window at her husband with a great concern look on her face she pulled the blinds back. And behold my grandfather stood at the edge of the lake with his fishing rod stretched out across the water shouting and praying asking God to divide the waters. The waters stood still just like it always had. Mud dirt catfish turtles and snakes filled the cold waters. The lake ignored the sounds of my grandfather's voice and stood still not even a breeze brushed across the waters that day. The lake stood still. Feet soaked in mud and mind overtaken by disillusion my grandfather came in the house angry and shame and said,

"It didn't part this time but I know I'm a prophet." Things like this went on for many days after that. Two weeks went by and he had gotten worst rather than better. It was no doubt in our minds my grandfather had appeared to have had a nervous breakdown. My grandmother was called off her job one night because my grandfather had stayed up all night preaching saying that he was a prophet. For two days straight he did not sleep he would not rest until he felt the acceptance from someone that would believe that he was what he said he was. Without a chose she had to call the hospital and have him admitted. How could this be, this sanctified Pentecostal preacher who was pastoring his own church get to this place in life? His breakdown affected the family and the church greatly. No one knew what had happened to get him to this point in his life. We questioned God and questioned him. Had he sinned? Had he gotten himself involved with the wrong people? What was wrong? Some said it was because he had gotten too involved in the church and his religion and all this Holy Ghost stuff caused him to finally snap. Then there were others that said, "no its not that at all, its because he didn't get enough of the Holy Ghost, He needs more of Jesus!" Which side was right? Did he have too much Jesus? Did he not have enough of Jesus? Many years passed and my grandfathers mind grew stronger and his life became a little better. He continued to preach and pray for those that were lost in life. He worked hard in the church until his physical health failed him. But after all those years the questions remained, what happened to my grandfather on that cool autumn day of 1986? A year before he passed and went home to be with the Lord I remember sitting around watching television with him and out of the blue he said, "boy, take life easy." I replied, "yes sir I'll do my best." He went on to say, "Make sure you do that now, because it gets hard and we don't know what the end may look like." As he seat there with his legs crossed and his thumb pressed against his cheek he cut his eyes at me and said, "fear can be your worst enemy. It well make your life hard." He said, "that's how I lost my mind all them years ago. I did not take life easy and fear overtook me. I was so scared that no one was going to believe in me or accept me as a real man of God so I started doing crazy things trying to prove something to folk that didn't care about me." The conversation that afternoon lasted a long time. He did most of the talking and I did all the listening. I learned that he had suffered from mental illness way before the fall of 1986. He told me that in the early 1960s he had been overtaken by fear. Thoughts of death hunted him day and night. He went on to tell me that he could not even drive pass a Hurst or a funeral home without breaking down crying. Anxiety and fear had taken complete control of his life and the only way he could be untethered from this tormenting force that maltreated him day and night was to adjoin himself to a higher power and obtain a greater faith in God. So in that year he gave his life to Christ. The moment he did that he said, "All that crazy stuff left my head and it left my life."

My beloved brothers and sisters I write to you to assure you that the love of God through faith will annihilate all fear in your life. Fear carries a great darkness with it, hiding the truth of who you really are. Blowing out the light of your faith it leads you into indistinct territory. All of the negative things that ever happened to us escorted a fear in our life and that fear caused us to go through life guarded. Trying to protect ourselves from pain. Please know that us humans are bad at covering ourselves. This has been a fact since the beginning of time. In Genesis three the Bible lets us know that Adam was engulfed by fear once he took the forbidden fruit from Eve his wife. Knowing that he was naked he covered himself along with his wife with fig leaves he hid in the garden. Notice here that he took something that did not produce life to cover him and free his shame because he was afraid. Fear causes us to connect with thing that do not give us life it is and apron of shame and embarrassment. "Who told you that you were naked?" God asked Adam. This question rings out through the heavens into the earth. Who told you that you were naked? Who told you that you wasn't covered? Who told you that you was a nobody? Who told you that you were not good enough? Who told you that you did not have purpose? Who told you that this is all life has to offer you? Who told you such things? The enemy will cause you to see your weaknesses and once it is revealed fear is birthed and when fear has taken it position, we began to cover and hide. After covering and hiding for so long the fig leaves die and the raw authentic us is shown. This is what happened to my grandfather. He covered himself for a long time. Covered himself with church and ministry, covered himself with his occupation covered himself with family and friends and when these fig leaves died the broken shameful embarrassed man appeared. We called him crazy we thought he had lost his mind when all along he was revealing what had been hidden behind the fig leaves, a broken rejected man full of fear anger and resentment. And because it had not been dealt with it was now dealing with him. What you fail to confront will condemn you in the end. Deal harshly with your fears. Treat them like a bad child discipline it with the rod of faith and love and it will not rule over your soul. Fear is just the shadow of your faith every time your faith moves fear moves with it. You must not be distracted by the shadows but you must be aware of the light that the shadow is reflecting from. Do this and you will live. Fear will always be there but it is up to you to allow it to govern your mind. A mind governed by fear is a mind that cannot be trusted. It will always be lead into dark places. Those that are fear focused never make changes in life they never take risk. They are paralyzed from the soul all the way down to the spirit. They fail to make moves. They only move when it seems safe. Comfort is their faithful companion. So they ease their way through life. Scared to adjust, they sit on the stool stupidity. Not knowing the power that is within them. And once their lives are over and have come to an end and death has covered their body the memory of their existence is covered by death as well for no one will take memory of a fool who failed to face their fears. Life is never easy. Its full of pain fears and heartbreak but we must overthrow the dictatorship of these contrary abstracts replacing them with purpose, healing, and faith. Oh how I have seen the death of many dreams and the impotent potential of many men and women because of fear. They die never knowing who they really are. Great and powerful individuals have expired in the prime of their lives because they allowed comfort and fear to be their portion in life. They failed to see the light and made the shadows to take the lead role on the stage of their lives. Becoming blind to truth they lived a lie expecting things to just fall in place and when it did not happen for them their hearts were darken and the storm of life consumed them. Fear is that driving force that pushes you into depression anxiety and loneliness. It will cost you to lose your mind. I have never met a fearful man whose mind was not tormented. Fear must be dealt with and controlled by prayer and the word of God if you fail to do this you have failed in life. Become wise and face that which is ever confronting you. A foolish man runs from a fight that he know he can win but a wise man's battle will be won by his faith. My grandfather died a wise man. Realizing where he messed up and acknowledging where it all went wrong he made the adjustments. He faced his dysfunctions becoming fearless in the face of opposition. He never lost his faith. Although things did not work out the way he planned them he kept himself in faith and died in the faith knowing that fear was just an echo it had never been a voice. Many people mocked him and pocked fun at him after his mental breakdown but he never allowed their opinions to define his fate. He realized that there were always going to be people that did not believe in him and he refused to prove anything to them he never allowed that negative action to produce an everlasting fear. Never be afraid of the people around you, they can't harm you. The biggest threat to your future is not them but you. Stop looking for what those monsters are saying and find out who you are and listen to what God is saying. Charles Darwin once said, "We stopped looking for Monsters under our bed when we realized they were inside us." Rid yourself of the inward monster and embrace the faith you have on the inside it is your only defiance against fear. You my friend must own the fact that there will always be fear but it will not last for faith is eternal; but fear is temporal. Fear can not sit in the presence where faith is standing. Power, love, and a sound mind will forever be the reward of the faithful but the fearful will have no position in the habitations of success. Fight your way through cry your way through push shove press your way if you must, but whatever you do, do not fear. We all have our fears and we all must face them but whatever you do not let it win. It's a lie, it never produces truth. Its purpose is to stop you from transforming into a greater and better you. If you have to lose your mind to find your faith so be it but never allow fear to speak or have any say in whatsoever you do. Your life is precious handle it with faith your life is fragile hold it gently with love your life is significant embrace it daily with care. Know that you are being held up by a higher power by a force and a being that does not share equal ground with fear but rather defeats it. If you can see the invisible you can do the impossible.

CHAPTER 7

WATCH YOUR MOUTH

＋＋＋＋＋＋

Death and life are in the power of the tongue:

and they that love it shall eat the fruit thereof.

—Proverbs 18:21, King James Version

Hurling out of the galaxies the voice of God stepped onto the platform of darkness and void and begin to create. Darkness became powerless before his presence when He opened His mouth and said, "let there be light!" The sun quickly took her position and hung in space and the darkness bowed before it. God stood back and gave Himself praise knowing that what he had spoken was good. Separating the clouds from the water He lifted the fog into the heavens and created the sky. His spirit filled the atmosphere as mountains and plains grew out of the sea and He called the dry ground land and stepped back and took a real good look at what he had done and praised Himself again. Let there be seed and vegetation bearing plants and fruit, let it come up out of the ground. Then the voice of God walked through the land

and fruit bearing trees and vegetation and vines pierced through the ground. God looked and saw that what he had spoken once again was good and He praised Himself yet again for His words were not failing. After creating the birds in the air and the creatures of the land and sea He looked around at the heavenly host that had been surrounding and watching Him do His best work He said, "Let's make man, lets make him in our image and after our likeness. The heavens agreed and God began to make man. Blowing into the dust of the land what seemed to be a sand storm the hand of God moving about in the eye of wind storm lightning flashed and an image appeared and when the dust was settled there laid man and God breathed into his nostrils and the breath of God created the soul of man and the man moved freely about the garden walking and talking like God in the image of God creating and speaking like God, naked but yet not ashamed for he was covered by the presence of the Almighty God.

Out of all the creatures and living things that move and breath upon the earth the human being is the most unique creature ever. What sets us apart from the others is that we are a living soul. Beyond having desires emotions and intellect we have the ability to speak. No other creation was organized or invented to do such thing. When God spoke and said let us make man in our image and in our likeness He was simply saying, "let us make something that can create and speak like us. The ability to create and speak is spiritual evidence that we have the Devine DNA of God generating through our being. Please know this my dear brothers and sisters that in the beginning when God created the heavens and the earth he didn't touch anything but he spoke and everything that was in Him came out of Him by the words of His mouth. Everything He had in mind He put it in His mouth and created it. In the beginning of creation the words "God said" is mentioned ten times. The number ten symbolizing Gods perfect will and purpose for life. So everything He said was good and very good perfected by the words that came out of His mouth. And His will concerning us is that we reflect Him in the earth. Notice that God didn't speak about what he saw around Him but He spoke out what He didn't see around Him. It was darkness around Him but notice He didn't magnify the presence of darkness by recognizing and honoring it but He called those things that be not and they were. (Romans 4:17) So many times we talk about what we see and we give it much attention. We often glorify the problem and disqualify the solution. For some reason we have tapped into this negative energy called complaining hiring the chaos we create storms and become angry when it rains. If you don't like what you are seeing change what you are saying. When God said, "let there be light" The sun was hired and became Gods employee to the earth and has never been terminated from its job because God created it to be good. Whatsoever you say you create and give power to. Your words send out invitations into the universe to form that which you speak. What are you inviting into your world? What have you said that made you who you are today? You are where you are because of what you said or did not say. Your position in life hangs on the words that fall out of your mouth.

At the age of twelve years old my grandfather and his uncle would take me to go and pick peaches with them. We worked for a white man who was a God fearing man and kind to all of those he came in contact with. For many years my grandfather and his uncle worked for him and was paid decent money and they would give me about five percent of what they made which added up to be about twenty dollars a day. That was a lot of money to me at that age and during that time period.

The sun was bearing hard on us that summer in the peach orchard. The fruits were ripe and ready to harvest. Reaching up at the top of the tree on the tip of my toes I stood trying to pursue the biggest but yet ripe peach I could see. "Get'em from the top, Get'em from the top!" Uncle shouted. Everything he said he said it twice. My grandfather and I were hot itching and tired from the labor decided to take a break and load the peach filled boxes onto that old 1970 Ford truck uncle had. This summer day in SouthGeorgia was filled with unbearable heat with very low humidity and the wind refuse to blow. The heat was unmovable it refused to yield its power. While loading the truck we heard uncle coughing uncontrollably. We found him leaning over a dead peach tree that had fallen in the field coughing and gasping for air he began to unbutton his shirt we handed him cool water to drink thinking that he had been overtaken by the heat and was growing faint but it was the last whooping cough that came out of him that we knew

that this reaction was much bigger than the weather around us. For it
was in the last cough that he spit up chunks of blood. Blood came out
his mouth falling to the ground like the rotten peaches that had let go
of the branches it was connected to around us. "MAN" My grandfather
said with a concern look on his face, "what have you gotten yourself
into that you puke up blood like this here?" Uncle straighten up and
leaned back and cut his eyes at my grandfather and said, "Well Red I
guess you ought to know, the doctor told me that I have lung cancer
and that I only have a few months to live. My grandfather and I stood
back in amazement and a hush came across the orchard not even the
sounds of tractors and mowers that we so often heard in the field they
became mute at the news and the words that came out of my uncle's.
And a small breeze moved slowly but yet briefly across the orchard at
that moment. "Well what you gone do?" my grandfather asked, "Awe
Hell Red I'm gone live!" He replied sharply. "These doctors don't know
what they talking about. They do not have know knowledge or power
more than what the good Lord gave them. My times is in the hand of
the Man upstairs and I believe if He tell me to live then I'm gone tell
myself to live and I be damn Red I'm gone live!" This Methodist deacon
had tapped over into a revelation about God and His people that we
(my grandfather and I) Pentecostal preachers had yet to tap into. This
was in 1991. The doctors told uncle that he wasn't going to live to see
Christmas. But because my uncle refused to submit to the confession
and diagnosis of the doctor he lived to see about ten more Christmases

after that. The more they spoke death the more he spoke life the more the doctors told him about his cancer the more he told them about how good he was feeling. The more they warned him about his illness the more he cursed them and rejected their methods of belief. My uncle lived. Having buried all of his siblings and his wife he stopped speaking and gave up the ghost and died. Being of a great age. If I am not mistaken He didn't even die because of the cancer He died from old age. This my friend is what I call the art of believing and speaking. Although my uncle wasn't a Pentecostal fire baptized apostolic believer like myself he believed in the power of the tongue.

As I look across this new generation of creators and believers I see people that are silent when it comes to speaking faith and life but loquacious when it comes to speaking facts and failure. We master in the minor things holding back life we refuse to speak out the positive. Your words are like seed when you speak out you give life to what you are saying and if you continue to say it eventually it will become your reality. Your life moves in the direction of your words. If you have a poor mouth you're going to have a poor life. But if your mouth is in agreement with the mouth and words of the Almighty then your life will be filled with great success and strength to stand any storm that comes your way. If you don't like what you are seeing then stop saying what you been saying. Stop speaking defeat and expecting victory. My brothers and sisters don't you know that no fountain can bring for sweet water and salt water at the same time? (James 3:11) Be stable and stubborn in your faith. Allowing no one to stir you into a life of disorder. Whatever you are in you can come out of it. All you have to do is open your mouth and use your words. Stop going through with your mouth shut. You don't win fights by being mute you win by believing and speak that which you know is true. Stop using your words to describe the situation but use your words to change the situation.

Ezekiel 37 King James Version (KJV), The hand of the Lord was upon me, and carried me out in the spirit of the Lord, and set me down in the midst of the valley which was full of bones, 2 And caused me to pass by them round about: and, behold, there were very many in the open valley; and, lo, they were very dry. 3 And he said unto me, Son of man, can these bones live? And I answered, O Lord God, thou knowest.

4 Again he said unto me, Prophesy upon these bones, and say unto them, O ye dry bones, hear the word of the Lord.

5 Thus saith the Lord God unto these bones; Behold, I will cause breath to enter into you, and ye shall live:

6 And I will lay sinews upon you, and will bring up flesh upon you, and cover you with skin, and put breath in you, and ye shall live; and ye shall know that I am the Lord.

7 So I prophesied as I was commanded: and as I prophesied, there was a noise, and behold a shaking, and the bones came together, bone to his bone.

8 And when I beheld, lo, the sinews and the flesh came up upon them, and the skin covered them above: but there was no breath in them.

9 Then said he unto me, Prophesy unto the wind, prophesy, son of man, and say to the wind, Thus saith the Lord God; Come from the four winds, O breath, and breathe upon these slain, that they may live.

10 So I prophesied as he commanded me, and the breath came into them, and they lived, and stood up upon their feet, an exceeding great army.

11 Then he said unto me, Son of man, these bones are the whole house of Israel: behold, they say, Our bones are dried, and our hope is lost: we are cut off for our parts.

12 Therefore prophesy and say unto them, Thus saith the Lord God; Behold, O my people, I will open your graves, and cause you to come up out of your graves, and bring you into the land of Israel.

13 And ye shall know that I am the Lord, when I have opened your graves, O my people, and brought you up out of your graves,

14 And shall put my spirit in you, and ye shall live, and I shall place you in your own land: then shall ye know that I the Lord have spoken it, and performed it, saith the Lord.

Take note here in the scripture that God placed the prophet in the mist of a dead and dry place among dead and dry people. And told him to speak to them. He spoke out what He did not see physically but once he spoke it came forth. Whatever you say it will come forth. I do believe that the creator is telling us to do the same. Whatever you see around you that's not matching up to what God showed you speak what you want it to be and you will see what you want it to be. Many times we curse our own lives by speaking doubt and unbelief. If my uncle would have spoken about his issue and agreed with the diagnosis of the doctor he would have died that year. If Ezekiel would have spoken to the bones telling them how defeated and dried up they were there would have never stood before him and exceedingly great army. But because they tapped into their God DNA and created life with their words they saw victory in the presence of defeat. What you say matters. Stop calling yourself dumb, stop complaining and saying how bad your life is and start speaking to it. Be the prophet of your life. Prophecy to yourself and call forth what you want it to be and it will come forth and it will be good and very good. Speak light where there is darkness, speak strength where there is weakness, speak prosperity where there is poverty, speak life where there is death. And the universe will set itself in order and submit to what you say. Your mouth is the most strongest thing you have on your body for it controls what's in you and dictates what's around you. Watch what you say. Be careful of the words that come out of your mouth for they are life and they are death.

CHAPTER 8

WORK

+ + + + + +

But wilt thou know, O vain man, that faith without works is dead?

-James 2:20, King James Version

Fingers cut and blistered from the thorns of the cotton cloves, small drops of blood landed on the cotton smeared with the DNA of slaves the bag became full and ready to be carried off and manufactured. Beads of sweat appeared on the forehead running down their face falling off the brown sun-kissed skin on to the ground like brown dry leaves off of a tree on a windy autumn day. No time to rest no moment to break, from sun up to sun down work was the abusive spouse of the slave and the forced company of the Black American Negro. Many lacked knowledge of many things all they ever knew was work. It controlled every part of their being. My grandfather did not even know his ABCs he could barely read and the only thig he could write was his name. All he knew was work. Working the field picking cotton, picking peas, picking corn, cutting down sugar cane, plowing the field and working the farm. Being or doing anything else as a black uneducated man was taboo. Having eight children he only made about four dollars a day which added up to be twenty dollars a week. Poverty shielded my family for years it was a wall of death keeping out anything that would cause prosperity and life. No matter how hard or how long they would work it was never enough to overcome or to come over the wall of lack and destitute. Oh how we quote the scripture, "The love of money is the root of all evil." (1st Timothy 6:10) but no one talks about how evil and wicked poverty can be. Poverty is evil alone. It doesn't need company it doesn't need and enabler although a slack and slothful hand will usher in its presence its coming needs no announcement when poverty shows up its presence will speak loud and clear and once it has been heard it will destroy every part of your life and dismiss happiness from the mist of your home. Poverty carries no mercy it will kill a working man, it will leave wives widowed screaming and crying in the streets, it will starve a baby to death, it will leave an innocent man in prison without a trial it will make an honest man lie, it will cause a loving man to cheat and steal, it will cause a faithful man to fall and give up. the hand of poverty will lead those that are sick to the doors of death and the grave. The wrath of poverty will leave dead bodies in the street to rot unburied and unbothered it will cause the best of friends to become the worst of enemies. Poverty is ruthless wicked in every part its very nature is to steal kill and to destroy. And the only potency to defeat this evil abstract is work and faith. These two are the only power that can eliminate the existence of poverty. Work and faith together is a mighty duo that no earthly being can terminate. For with these two partnered together obtains the answer to all things, weapons of mass destruction.

August of 1619 the first slave ship landed in Jamestown Virginia. Slumped over weak and frail weary from the long ship ride the slaves were auctioned off branded and sold and put to work in the fields and some in houses. Hired on a job that only paid beating, blood sweat, torture and death. Given only enough to survive they became property but yet treated worst than the land they worked on. All that work and no pay all that labor and no reward but it was when the slaves were introduced to a faith that their world began to change, and their work began to pay off. Taught pure scripture yet polluted by the master to excuse his on bigotry and injustice of the black human race. Although it was against the law to teach a slave to read and write many were taught and it was in this that power was produced. For in the same bible that taught, "Slaves obey your master."

(Colossians 3:22) also said, ' I have surely seen the affliction of my people and have heard their cry by reason of their taskmasters; for I know their sorrow and I am come down to deliver them (Exodus 3:7&8). This book that was talking to the bound was also speaking to the master saying, "set them free." It was in that moment that faith stirred up in the negro man and the negro woman and poverty had to lose its holt. Although it took many many years to see the pay off, pay day finally came. Your faith must have works and your works must have faith and these two are constructed by education. We often suffer because we fail to work and we fail to work because we fail to believe that the work we put out is not good enough and we fail to believe because we simply just don't know that what lies ahead of us is freedom and land a of better living.

A lazy man is not always a man that don't want to work sometimes it's the man that's just been hurt. It's a man that gave up when he didn't see the fruit of his labor, it's a man that was placed under so much pressure that he fail to believe that things were going to get better so he became a slave to poverty, working hard to get nothing or simply just not working at all because all of his energy and ambition has been beat out of him and starved to death by those who failed to free him. You can't be that man. You can't be that woman.

You must educate yourself and allow that to build a faith in you that will drive you to work your way out of every obstacle that comes your way. Get up get out of the bed stop looking at television all day wishing and hoping that better will come your way. Stop praying and asking God in His sovereignty to do what you can do in your humanity. You can't live your life wanting people to do for you what you know you can do for yourself. You are so much greater than that bed you are laying on, you are so much better than that job you have allowed yourself to get stuck on. Success do not come to those that take the easy way and the lazy way out it only comes to those that work and believe. Procrastination is the poison that slothful men drink that preeminent them to indigence. They wait until its too late to start moving drunken off of the poison they think like fools becoming unprepared unable and unwanted they are absent at the table of success. Putting rest before work, sleep before labor, relaxation before movement and when others succeed, they become envy and jealous and the seed of Cain settles in their hearts ready to destroy the faith and works of his brother. Procrastination is your greatest enemy and the biggest threat to your success kill it with determination. Pressure is the only cure for those who have been poisoned by procrastination. Allow yourself to feel the pressure of your family needing you and wanting you to succeed, feel the pressure of lack at your backdoor knocking wanting to come in and if you take a nap now he may just break in and take everything you have. Take on the pressure that this next generation needs you and if you give a slack hand now it may handicap those that are following in your footsteps. No more wasting your time. Do what needs to be done.

(A man who dares to waste one hour of time has not discovered the value of life -Charles Darwin) You have taken enough time off and wasted precious time doing things that are irrelevant to your future. Life happens to us all. We all have done crazy stupid things that brought us to a dead-end in life trust me I get it. But you cannot allow those things to stop your faith and break your hands from working you must reach beyond yourself and give life all you got. The strength of a thousand men are in you, the power of a hundred lightning bolts are shooting through your fingertips you just have to work it and most of all believe it. The days of procrastination is over the days of excuses have come to an end. You have been hurt long enough you have thought about healing and prosperity long enough now is the time to get up and go get what is rightfully yours. How long will you keep going like this how long will you keep allowing the failure and pain to dictate the power that is with in you? Don't you know that your faith and your ability to work will bring you freedom in every area of your life? Add faith to your works. Work alone will only bring frustration and loneliness it has no power when it is absent from the presence of faith. No matter how much money you make you will never be satisfied for it is your faith that will bring you into complete wholeness. Work without faith will cause you to obtain what you want but in the end, it will make you beg for what you need. Put your faith in the mix and it will bring your life into full complete happiness. This faith comes by education. The Apostle Paul would say it like this, "faith comes by hearing and hearing by the word of God." (Romans 10:17) what you hear creates what you see in yourself and what you see in yourself shapes what you see around you. Its this type of faith that gave my ancestors strength to make it through the beatings and hangings it was this faith that my people stood on when their families were busted up and sold off. This faith gave us a song in the field, this faith gave us a hymn in the face of Jim Crow, and it is this faith that will continue to lead us into greater victory. The same faith and the same energy to work that brought us this far is the same faith and work that will bring great success. I missed out on great opportunities because of my failure to add work to my faith. I had many bad days because I failed to believe God more than I believed in a job. Please understand that because you have a job does not mean you are working. You can be busy doing a whole lot of nothing. Movement does not equal productivity. If you are moving, make sure you are going somewhere. Set a goal set a deadline and make sure you get there. You cannot allow the last years of your life to look like the former years of your life. Be productive. If you are working, make sure it adding to your life and to the lives of others. That is where the peace is and the joy of living is tangible, when you are adding to the lives of others in a positive way. True happiness is found in helping others. Your job as a human being is not fulfilled until you have made someone's life better and easier. Never forget that. Do not get stuck in the field working for the master only to get paid with beatings sweat blood and death. Your life is so much more than that. Find you! Find yourself in faith and watch how amazing your life will become. My mother is the hardest working woman I will ever know. She worked in the hospital for years cleaning the floors and washing the windows making little to nothing just to make ends meet. How she provided for my brother and I, I just do not know. After 15years of housekeeping she transferred to radiology transport department and it was then I saw her faith come alive. She would pray day and night calling on the name of the Lord and I tell you the truth my beloved friends God heard her and blessed her. I always admired my mother for her hard work in the marketplace and in ministry. Mama is a fire baptized holiness praying preacher a true evangelist. I love that about her. She was the one that put faithfulness and good work ethics in me. My mother was not in me and my brother's life much because she dedicated her life to her job and to the church and God and nothing came before it. She would go homeless before she stops paying her tithes her faith in God has always been unshakeable. When she gave her life to God there was no turning back. No, she isn't perfect but she works very hard at it. She has been my biggest inspiration in life and my biggest motivation in ministry. The epitome of faith and works. She is a living witness that faith will work for you if you work it. I have learned to set my heart towards believing God even when its not popular. My faith has carried me through many nights and walked with me many days. I challenge you to grab hold to that faith and never let go. Hold on to it until it starts holding on to you. Become daring and fearless. Never take no for an answer work hard as you can, take very few breaks, believe as hard as you can and never slack up in your faith for it is there where all the freedom and happiness lies. You are no longer a slave but a freeman, working hard and smart obtaining what is rightfully yours. Your coming out of the fields into faith and off from under the taskmaster into a land of prosperity. You may have some rough days and times may get hard, but your faith will sustain you and your works will build you an everlasting legacy.

CHAPTER 9

IT WON'T BE THIS WAY ALWAYS

-----------◆◆◆◆◆◆------------

Many are the afflictions of the righteous: but the

Lord delivereth him out of them all.

-Psalm 34:19, King James Version

Molested, dyslexic, fatherless, ill tempered, suicidal, and depressed these are the words that once defined me. Born into a broken home, statistics would say I would be in jail, in a gang or in the grave. I was born with the odds stacked against me, being a black male in America alone has its own burden. But somehow, I made it. Many nights I cried wondering why God allowed so much pain to be on me. I knew what Sofia meant when she said, "all my life I had to fight!" (Alice Walker the Color Purple 1984) The line in that movie was a joke and a laughing matter to many but to me it was a reality. I had to fight in every area of my life and to be very honest with you I got tired. I got tired of fighting, I got tired of being hit and being rejected, I got tired of being looked down on and ignored because I did not have, I got tired of living. Life was too hard. Molested for years made to feel like a worthless nobody. Not knowing what love really was and not knowing how to really love. All I knew was pain. I got tired of pain. Pain had worn out her welcome it was time for her to go! I did not know how she was leaving and where she was going but I knew one thing, she had to get out of my life. So, I poured myself in church and in ministry and the load I was carrying became a little lighter. Got married young had nothing at all not even a decent job. The chaotic life that was offered to me from a child now I was connecting another beautiful human being to this dysfunction. I did not know anything just a country boy from South Georgia who wanted to be a good preacher. How could he be a good preacher when everything he ever had as a child was bad? Although pain seemed to be ever present in my life there was something on the inside of me that would provoke me to keep going. Even when we lived in a motel, I could hear a small voice say, "better days are coming." Sleeping on my mother's living room floor in her one bedroom apartment that voice would visit me in the night when I would be crying and tears rolling over the side of my nose on to my pillow, that voice would say, "don't worry things are going to change." When I had to dissolve my church and the owner put the locks on the door and I was no longer a pastor and had to sit under leaders that looked down on me, I could hear that small voice say, "If you can make it through this life is going to get better." It was during these times I just want to die I didn't want to live at all. I was embarrassed ashamed and condemned. Looking at the others prosper brought great depression on me but yet I held my head up high. I smiled and I shouted, and I danced even when I wanted to quit. One night while I was preaching in Alabama, I had grew tired and sad. I could no longer hear that voice speaking to me it had vanished away with everything I lost and everyone that left me. I wept bitterly that night. In the mist of my pity party I got a call from a pastor in Chicago. I answered the phone delicately but yet strong and the voice on the other end of that phone spoke to me very firmly and said, "what's wrong? Talk to me." I began to cry and tell him all about the pain and trials I was facing and I repeated to him over and over that I just wanted to give up and that I had nothing to live for I was all out of hope and most all I was all out of faith. He replied with such grace. With a gentle voice he said to me, "If you honestly believe that life is over for you and that there is no more hope for you in the future, then you have my permission to give up. but if there is still a fire in you like I know it is, if there is a small spark of faith that is telling you that things are going to get better, I tell you truth you better hang on with everything you got because things are going to get better." It was then that I heard that voice coming back to life in me. Comforting me and letting me know that there was so much to live for, and life was not over by a long shot. I broke down that night, but I also broke through. The power to fight and to believe was revived and I stood strong. So much has happened to me so many rose up against me and so many mistakes I made but I never allowed it to stop me. I preached many days depressed

I ran many revivals and conferences while being homeless. Some nights I left the church not knowing where I was going to lay my head, but God provided. Slept in my car with my family in the Walmart parking lot for days but I still showed up for church gave in the offering and lead the congregation in worship. Days I allowed the pressure of it all to lead me to do strange and sinful things trying to ease the pain of my present struggle. I would lie and cheat to find some type of peace or self fulfilment but in the end, it only brought me more pain. All I ever wanted was to be loved. Can somebody please love me? Can someone please care for me and help me? Don't judge me don't reject me don't hurt me, love me. These are the words that would ring in my spirit as a child and quake through my soul as an adult. When you have unresolved childhood pain it leaves you bitter. You force pain on the innocent, and you hurt others unintentionally. Making an excuse for every bad decision you find yourself becoming the very thing that was forced upon you. Fighting to be heard you suffer in silence when you are rejected and that leads to self-destruction. When you have not been loved properly real love is foreign. Although I had a loving wife and the most beautiful family their love wasn't enough because I had wholes in my soul and all the love and care they would bestow upon me leaked out of me leaving me unfulfilled and nothing was good enough. It was not until I found peace within myself that I realized how much I had abused me just like the others did. Life has a way of making you bow to its endless pain and deadly positions at your most lonely stage. Having lost it all I had no one to turn to but God. It was then that the love for myself was made known. I had to learn to love me. I had to learn to forgive me and to forgive those that hurt me and walked away from me I had to love me if no one else would I had to do it for myself. And when that happened everything I needed and wanted began to gravitate to me. It was as if God was unloading Heaven on my soul. The peace that came with it all was far more than money it was priceless. In spite of my mistakes and flaws God was still calling me to be His man. His love captured me at place that I thought would have killed me. I thought He had forgotten about me, I thought he did not need me anymore. I had messed up so bad who would want to love an outcast such as I. I didn't love me, I felt like they didn't love me but he made it known that he loved me and that my days of being alone and broken had ended and He had been there all along wanting to take the pain away. I had to let go of it all and when I did, He rescued me from it all.

Is that you? Are you hurting feeling like its over? Are you the one that carry a smile even when you are hurting? Have you ever been that person that seems to be blamed for every bad thing that ever happen? Are you running from your past? Are you finding it hard to let go of all the pain and hurt that was bestowed upon you in your life? Is that you? If so, I have good news for you. Trouble do not last always. You are going to make it. There is so much more to you than the pain you feel deep down inside. I know you are lonely, and no one understands the pressure and heartache you feel from day to day but trust me my brother and my sister, things are going to get better! I could not read I could barely speak proper English I was the black skinny feminine looking boy nobody wanted to be around. But I made it. I was in a mental institute twice in my life called crazy and demented. But I made it. If I can make it, I know you can make it. I know its hard, LIFE IS HARD! All you have to do is believe. If you learn to believe in, you again and believe in God I promise you things will get better. If God does not change things around you trust me when I tell you, He will change you around everything and the latter is always greater than the former. Do not give up, better days are ahead. Your life is about to change for the better. What you are facing now and what you have faced back then is only building character in you. It making you greater better and more powerful than you ever been. God is with you His hand is on you.

This Special Ed student became a Special Ed teacher. This dyslexic boy became a college student. This homeless man became an independent business owner. A peach picking Georgia country boy became a Pentecostal preacher. Who would have thought that me, who had two nerves breakdowns would become an advocate for mental illness helping others find their righteous mind? God knew. He promised me that days would get better and they did. Oh no I haven't arrived, I haven't arrived at all I have such a long way to go but I know that through each test and trial that I face from day to day that He is with me and everything I'm facing won't last forever and He'll make sure I come out on top. Whatever you do, do not fold under pressure.

Fight until you win. Keep swinging until you get the victory. You are not alone there is a winner in you, and He can only be seen when you give life your best shot. Give it your best shot and nothing I mean nothing will be held from you. You are undeniable, undefeatable, and victorious that is you at the core of your very being. Tough times do not last tough people do; you can come out no matter what you are going through.

CHAPTER 10

ITS ALL NEW NOW

+ + + + + +

Therefore if any man be in Christ, he is a new

creature: old things are passed away;

behold, all things are become new.

-2 Corinthians 5:17, King James Version

I had just left a leadership conference when some friends of mine and I were headed home. While on the road we stopped at the traffic light. While the car came to a slow holt we heared voices yelling out and crying from across the street. It wasn't a cry of pain but the cry of prayer. The voices of the saints floated through the wind bouncing off the buildings of that Westside Atlanta plaza. We turned down the radio and began to follow the sound. It was an old rundown gas station parking lot; there we found the missionairies praying in a circle. Their long skirts and head coverings flapping in the air as their voices cried out to God. In the circle were homeless men and women, drug addicts, alcholics, and winos. We pulled into that small broken parking lot jumped out of the car and ran to the prayer circle like a child runing into the arms of a loving guardine. Joining hands with these women we lifted our voices and prayed too. Crying and weeping as the power of Jesus Christ overtook us. People were driving by slowly to see what was going on traffic began to build at the sound of the saints. Those streets had heard gunshots, it heard the voices of mothers crying over their murdered child, those streets had seen drug transactions, rape, human trafficing but never had it seen or heared the cries of the Saints of God praying in the street. The atmosphere shifted in that moment. You could feel the darkness of that region backing down, the mouths of demonic influence was shut up and the Heavens opened up over us paralyzing the principality of that area. We called on the name of the Lord that day and nothing could stop us. With our eyes closed tight squeezing the hand of the person we were connected to in the circle we cried out for change. The voice of the church mother was so loud it moved like a frate train when she opend her mouth. Without a microphone or an amplifier her voice drove through that rundown area. Her spirit and her sound carried us to God. Our hearts were one at that moment. We didnt know each others name that was not important to us only one name got the attention that cool summer afternoon and that was the name of Jesus. As the prayer came to an end the circle that was nitted together by ten people had grown to over twenty indivisuals. The prayer alarm of the saints had gathered people from everywhere and those that were not in the circle stood off afar looking and watching us carry on like saints do. Leaping and jumping clapping our hands speaking in tongues enjoying the presence of God in public outside the four walls of a church building. With tears streaming down our face trempling under the presence of the Holy Ghost we let go of one anothers hand and huged and kissed one another as though we were at a family reunion. The old church mother grabbed me and hugged me very tight. She stood to be about five feet four but her spirit man was about ten feet five. She embraced me roughly and said, "you the one man of God, you hear me? You are the one. God's hand is on you. The world will know your name and many will be saved under the sound of your voice and because of your story." The next few words that came out of her mouth wrapped around my soul like a python wrapping around its prey before he devours it. She said, "Son God is not looking at your ability but your availability. Your ability may be valuable and great but your availabilty to Him is even greater." She slapped her hand on my forehead and began to speak in her heavenly lauguage and something like warm oil flowed over me in that parking lot. She pulled me by my shirt close to her so close I could smell the rose perfume she had clothed herself with and she said, "young man make the proper changes in your life and God will make the proper changes for your life." My friends and I left that public prayer meeting charged up and excited about what God had done that afternoon. But little did they know what had happened to me in that beat up parking lot. A change had come over me. I knew then that nothing about my life would ever be the same. When I returned home that afternoon I was quiet and to myself. I wanted God more than anything a hunger for Him stirred up in me and every mistake I had made and every person I had wronged came before me and I repented to God and cried out to Him once again on that day only this time I was by myself in a private room just me and God I told God that day that I was ready to change and become a new me.

The only thing in the universe you can really change is yourself and you can not change what you refuse to confront and confronting yourself is not easy. It takes true humilty for one to chestize himself when he is wrong. Its hard changing your life. No one can do it for you I know you wish they could but they can't. You are responsible for you. Stop putting your life in the hands of those that cant change you and take control of the wheel of your life and drive yourself into success. I spent over thirty years looking for something that I had in me all along. I thought moving from state to state and ctiy to city would give me a new start but it only gave me a new surrounding with the same old problems. When you have been bound and chained to that which is a threat to your future you must realize that when God chooses to deliver you the chains dont fall off your surroundings but the chains must fall off of you. Before you can be freed out of it you must first become free in it. If you dont become free in it no matter where you go you will always be bound so find your freedom where you are right now before you move to the next place in life. Free yourself before you try and free your surroundings. We often pray and cry out to God to fix others when its God's desire to fix us.

One of the biggest enemies to your future is the old you. Please know that freedom and deliverance has nothing to do with your geographic location but it has everything to do with who you are as a person. Old you must die so that new you can live. Stop changing jobs and changing cities and lovers and get stable and change you! Nothing will change until you change, and the quicker you become free in it the faster you can come out of it. We all like new things but very few want to pay for the new things. I am so sorry to tell you this but the new you is not free, its going to cost you. To become fresh and new its going to cost you the old you. You must die to all that you have known and all that you have obtained and count it as nothing and then and only then you will be able to succeed like you never have before. Give it up and walk away from it even if you have to walk away empty handed. I tell you the truth, its not going to be easy but its going to be worth it, for what once was will never be greater than what will be. The best version of you is not behind you but ahead of you. I dont care how old you are God will never allow your past to be greater than your future when you trust Him. Its all new now, you are no longer a victim but you are victorius. So many came up against you and some may be fighting against you now but that doesnt matter anymore because you have overcome them. You have proven that they all are liars. What once held you back is now holding you up. Your pain is now your platform a new and improved you has emerged out of the ashes. No one has the power over you but God. Its been a long time coming but you made it. Its not what you thought it would look like but day by day God is reintroducing Himself to you and revieling a new and better you to the the world. Stop your crying cancel your pity party hold your head up high walk into the room like you own it because you do. You are powerful beyond meassure nothing can stop you now. Look how far you come. You survived the worst you even did the worst but somehow you find yourself breathing and able to take on life another day. Its all new now, your life will never be the same, your life is going to a whole new level. Sometimes things have to get worst before they can get better but I tell you my beloved the worst is over and the best has come. The best version of you is holding this book right now. It may not feel like it it may not seem like it but you have evolved into something beautiful. Do you believe that? Blessed are you that believe these words I tell you for the words I tell you are true and truth always brings forth light and life. I gave up many days, i failed many times, but I kept trying even when they called me stupid and crazy. I gave life my best shot. If I died now I can say I gave life all I had even when life gave me nothing but heart ache and pain. I mastered getting up. I never allowed the negative to be the end of my story I lived through it to testify to you that things get better and your life will change as you go through changes but never let whats around you to dictate the faith you have in you. Keep that fire and passion to live burning deep in your soul and spring forth in the newness of life. All that you are and all that you ever will be is in you. The power of God is in you. This is the power that my grandmother told me about its the power that my mother pushed me into its that power that kept me from losing myself when I lost it all. You have that power too. All you have to do is pray seek God turn to Him. He is the answer He is that new life you been looking for, He is that one true love that you been longing for its in Him that all good things dwell and there is no darkness found in Him at all. I been to every conference I preached many revivals held many church services and had no peace until I dedicated my life to Him once and for all. I walked away from things looking good over into things being good. Do that and you too will find peace in it all. You are not forgotten you are not forsaken you have been remembered in the courts of Heaven and God is about to do you good. Its all new now nothing will ever be the same your life is about to make since. All of those who counted you out are about to wish they counted you in. You are ahead of them now, truth is you always have been, the veil of hardships in life wouldnt allow you to see it. The veil has been removed from your eyes and now you see that you been great all along. I allowed the negative jugment of others to control me. I allowed their words and thoughts of me to dictate my life. It caused me to walk in great fear I was a slave to their actions and their reactions until I saw the power that I reall had in me and when I saw it there was no changing me I had been exposed to greatness and once you been exposed to greatness you have zero tollarance for mundane living. This world system has been design to make you stop being the best you. But you must stand against it and fight for what you believe. Keep dreaming keep working keep winning and keep believing and nothing that is good will be kept away from you. Problems will come trials will knock at your door but you must not answer the door alone, make sure your faith is right beside you advicating. Everything is new now, you have no reason to go back to what you use to do and who you use to be. Your new life has conqueored the old you and now that it has been conqueored make sure it never rises again. Rebuke those that remind you of who you use to be and what you use to do. Let them know that the old you has passed away. Like the old church mother I am pulling you close and I'm telling you now; if you change your life God will make the changes for your life. I never seen that old church mother again but I know without a doubt that God sent her to me to provoke the power of change in me like I'm provoking the power of change in you. Nothing about you is simple or lame. Every part of you has been revived and has changed into a powerful undefeatable species. Not because you were the strongest of them all or the most gifted of all, not even because you were the most bright intellectual but you are powerful because you never allowed the changes arround you to change you into anything less than what you were called to be. Your availabilty to Him is growing stronger than your ability from Him and that is what is going to continue and cause you to evolve.

It is not the strongest of the species that survives, nor the most intelliegent that survives. It is the one that is the most adaptable to change, that lives within the means available and works co-operatively against common threats. -Charles Darwin

EPILOGUE

LET GOD IN

Behold, I stand at the door, and knock: if any

man hear my voice, and open the door,

I will come in to him, and will sup with him, and he with me.

-Revelation 3:20, King James Version

The house was dark that night the lights were out due to a thunderstorm that had taken place an hour before. Laying in bed next to my wife who was sound asleep. I was up on my phone scrolling through social media. Raindrops dripping from the sides of the house slowly as lightning flashed without the sound of thunder following proving to me that the storm was over. I laid there drifting off to sleep as the light of my phone shined on my face. The sound of feet shuffling in the dark was faint in my ear, the first couple of shuffles and stumbles I ignored. Then the sound of something fallen got my attention. I sat straight up in the bed gripping my phone tightly in my right hand my heart pounded thinking that there was an intruder in the house. The electricity popped on at my reaction to the sound. I eased my way through that small shotgun house. On my tiptoes I walked softly into the back room where the children laid quietly asleep. I peeked my head through the door and there laid four children sleep and covered up comfortably in bed. I quickly turned on the light and began to look in the closet and in the other room my heart was beating out of my chest because there were only four children in the room there was supposed to be five, my son was nowhere in sight. I ran outside in a panic yelling and screaming his name but there was no response. I ran back in the house looked in the room once again thinking that maybe he was hidden under the sheets. While searching violently but yet carefully for him, I heard someone stumbling in the bathroom I rushed to the door of the bathroom and called out my sons name he faintly replied; "daddy I am so sorry I made a mess." I said what is it son, what's wrong?" I made a mess in my sleep and it is everywhere, "I didn't mean to do it I don't feel so well," he groaned. I began to knock on the door and said, "son let me in." No daddy it is a mess, it's really bad I smell bad and I don't want you to see me like this," he cried. "Open the door son let me help you. It is ok I will clean you up and we can make it better." He open the door shamefully and I went in to where the mess was and I saw this thirteen year old boy sitting there ashamed afraid and sick and in need of my help. I put my hands on the soap and bath towel turned the shower on and I bathed my son cleaned him up washed his clothes and the sheets that he had soiled and got him new linen to lay on and fresh under garments to wear, hugged him told him that everything

100